THE PRECISIONIST VIEW IN AMERICAN ART

An exhibition organized by the Walker Art Center, Minneapolis   H. H. Arnason, Director

November 13 through December 25, 1960

In cooperation with

THE WHITNEY MUSEUM OF AMERICAN ART

THE DETROIT INSTITUTE OF ARTS

THE LOS ANGELES COUNTY MUSEUM

THE SAN FRANCISCO MUSEUM OF ART

THE PRECISIONIST VIEW

in American Art

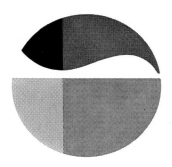

Ault

Blume

Crawford

Davis

Demuth

Dickinson

Driggs

Guglielmi

Hirsch

Lewandowski

Lozowick

O'Keeffe

Schamberg

Sheeler

Spencer

Stella

ACKNOWLEDGMENTS

*On behalf of the boards of directors and trustees of the Walker Art Center,
the Whitney Museum of American Art, the Detroit Institute of Arts, the
Los Angeles County Museum, and the San Francisco Museum of Art,
I would like to thank the many individuals and institutions who have
assisted in the preparation of this exhibition.*

*Important cooperation came from many of the artists themselves, and
Miss O'Keeffe, Mr. Sheeler, and Mr. Crawford were particularly generous in
giving their time in discussions. Because of her long and distinguished
association with many of the Precisionist artists, Mrs. Edith Gregor Halpert,
Director of The Downtown Gallery, was able to offer excellent advice and
assistance. Thanks are also due Mr. John I. H. Baur, Associate Director of
the Whitney Museum, for examining a detailed plan of the exhibition, and
Dr. Dmitri Tselos of the Department of Art, University of Minnesota, for
his thorough reading of the catalogue. Mr. H. H. Arnason, Director
of the Walker Art Center, has long been interested in presenting this
exhibition and offered valuable suggestions for its organization and catalogue.
Miss Doris Bry, because of her special knowledge of the Stieglitz collection
and her friendship with Miss O'Keeffe, made a considerable contribution
to this project. Not only did the William H. Lane Foundation make major
loans to the exhibition, but Mr. Lane, who has great enthusiasm for the
work of the Precisionists, gave generous and patient help in many details
of the exhibition's organization.*

*For providing important biographical and other information on the
Precisionist artists and their milieu, we are grateful to Mrs. Louise Ault,
Mr. Stephan Bourgeois, Mr. Alexander Brook, Mr. Paul Burlin, Mr. Charles
Daniel, Mr. Stuart Davis, Mr. Oronzo Gasparo, Mrs. O. Louis Guglielmi,
Mr. Hilaire Hiler, Mr. Douglas MacAgy, Mr. Henry McBride, Mrs.
Morton J. Meyers, Miss Dorothy C. Miller, Mr. Lewis Mumford,
Mr. Lee Nordness, Mr. Robert Schoelkopf, Jr., Mr. James Johnson Sweeney,
and Mr. William Zorach.*

*Important information was also provided by the Minneapolis Public Library,
the University Gallery of the University of Minnesota, and the libraries
and reference departments of the Columbus Gallery of Fine Arts, the Franklin
and Marshall College, Lancaster, Pa., the Solomon R. Guggenheim
Museum, the Museum of Modern Art, and the Whitney Museum. The
Archives of American Art at the Detroit Institute of Arts supplied
excellent documentation, through its remarkable microfilm program, on
virtually every artist represented in the exhibition.*

Color plates for Demuth's My Egypt *were generously lent by the Whitney
Museum and those for Sheeler's* Midwest *(made in cooperation with the
Walker Art Center) and O'Keeffe's* New York Night *by* Art in America.

I would also like to thank Art in America *for permission to include in the
catalogue essay material from my article on the Precisionists which appears
in the October, 1960 issue of that magazine. This special issue was planned
to coincide with the opening of the exhibition and contains a group of
articles by Edward Deming Andrews, H. H. Arnason, and Vincent J.
Scully, Jr., dealing with the Precisionist idea in architecture as well as in
the most recent American painting.*

*For preparation of the catalogue, particular thanks are due Mrs. Nancy
B. Miller of the Walker Art Center staff for her generous editorial assistance;
to Miss Donna Anderson and Mrs. Leah Corbin, staff secretaries,
for their patient attention to the many details of its assembly; to Miss Joan
Smith for her able handling of its registrarial aspects; and to Mr. Rob
Roy Kelly for its design.*

MARTIN L. FRIEDMAN
*Curator of the Walker Art Center
and Director of the Exhibition*

LENDERS TO THE EXHIBITION

ART MUSEUM OF THE NEW BRITAIN INSTITUTE; BALTIMORE MUSEUM OF ART; DR. AND MRS. MELVIN BOIGON; THE BROOKLYN MUSEUM; CALIFORNIA PALACE OF THE LEGION OF HONOR; MR. AND MRS. JOHN J. CARNEY; CITY ART MUSEUM OF ST. LOUIS; CLEVELAND MUSEUM OF ART; COLUMBUS GALLERY OF FINE ARTS; MR. RALSTON CRAWFORD; DETROIT INSTITUTE OF ARTS; THE DOWNTOWN GALLERY; FOGG ART MUSEUM, HARVARD UNIVERSITY; MRS. EDSEL B. FORD; GENERAL MOTORS RESEARCH LABORATORIES; MR. AND MRS. EDWARD S. GREENBAUM; MRS. EDITH GREGOR HALPERT; MR. AND MRS. BERNARD HEINEMAN, JR.; MR. JOSEPH H. HIRSHHORN; MR. AND MRS. MARTIN JANIS; MR. AND MRS. M. B. KAPLANSKY; WILLIAM H. LANE FOUNDATION; MR. AND MRS. MILTON LOWENTHAL; MR. LOUIS LOZOWICK; NORMA AND JOHN MARIN, JR.; THE METROPOLITAN MUSEUM OF ART; MILWAUKEE ART CENTER; MUSEUM OF FINE ARTS, BOSTON; MUSEUM OF MODERN ART; NEBRASKA ART ASSOCIATION; MR. AND MRS. ROY R. NEUBERGER; NEWARK MUSEUM; NORTON GALLERY AND SCHOOL OF ART; THE PHILLIPS COLLECTION; SAN FRANCISCO MUSEUM OF ART; DR. AND MRS. IRA LEO SCHAMBERG; SMITH COLLEGE MUSEUM OF ART; MR. AND MRS. STEPHEN A. STONE; WALKER ART CENTER; ANDREW DICKSON WHITE MUSEUM OF ART, CORNELL UNIVERSITY; WHITNEY MUSEUM OF AMERICAN ART; YALE UNIVERSITY ART GALLERY; ZABRISKIE GALLERY.

INTRODUCTION

This exhibition is a profile of one of the most significant directions in American art. Its artists have meticulously painted a remarkable complex of indigenous themes: colonial architecture, pristine farm-houses and barns, prairies and deserts untouched by "progress," and the great urban and industrial manifestations that for so long symbolized America to the world.

The exhibition is heavily weighted in its representation of works from the Twenties. Historically this is as it should be since in that decade the Precisionist premise was completely revealed, its themes and techniques were all in evidence.

In planning the exhibition, no attempt was made to show an equal number of works by each artist. Rather, it seemed reasonable to document in greater detail the development of those painters who throughout their mature careers adhered to Precisionist approaches. In recent years, virtually all the artists of the original Precisionist group have been presented in one-man exhibitions that have been thoughtful, objective documentations of their art; these are noted in the catalogue's biographical section.

The number of works included for each artist is not necessarily proportionate to his individual reputation but indicates the degree of his relationship to the Precisionist development. Thus the painting of Georgia O'Keeffe and Charles Sheeler receives the greatest attention in the exhibition and essay. These artists represent the essence and the heights of the movement. For Sheeler, architectural and mechanical themes have been central to his entire production. If purely architectural themes are a smaller part of O'Keeffe's painting, her unwaveringly "precise" approach to a unique iconography of botanical forms, landscapes, still lifes, and abstractions readily establishes her dominance in the movement.

Some artists were part-time Precisionists. Demuth, for example, is as well known for his watercolor still lifes, genre studies, and imaginative illustrations for the psychological novels of Zola, James, and Wedekind as for his austere Precisionist themes. Stuart Davis and Joseph Stella, unquestionably major figures in modern American painting, are represented by one work each to show important related directions and influences on the Precisionist idea.

Also, within the limits of the exhibition's size it was necessary to choose a group of artists whose work represents the maximum range of the style. This selection could easily be enlarged in a more detailed study: such artists as Francis Criss, Henry Billings, and Charles Goeller historically have been associated with the direction; many magic-realist painters, if technique alone were the determinant, could be considered Precisionists. The paintings of the ruler and compass geometricians who initially exhibited with the American Abstract Artists group are related and in many ways parallel to the non-figurative aspects of the Precisionist style. Significantly, on the basis of its sharply defined forms and controlled technique, even the newly emerging geometric-classicism, developed from the context of abstract expressionism, has been to a great extent anticipated by the Precisionist development.

Throughout the following essay there is reference to the extraordinary range of the Precisionist style. The photographic realism of O'Keeffe and Sheeler is frequently contrasted with their more abstract paintings. Such variation within the work of a single artist is characteristic of the movement. A conventional idea of realism does not apply to the Precisionists and these artists cannot be neatly divided into "realists" and "abstractionists." The fact is that the Precisionist attitude is fundamentally a realistic one. In this movement, style is secondary to attitude and these painters, regardless of their degree of departure from objective appearances, base their art on the objective world.

M. L. F.

To the memory of Edgar Craig Schenck (1909-1959)

THE PRECISIONIST VIEW IN AMERICAN ART

BEGINNINGS

From the current vantage point of American painting, the Precisionist phenomenon appears as if seen through the reverse end of a telescope — its reduced image is at once isolated, remote, and even nostalgic. New styles have succeeded each other with such frequency as almost to obscure the fact that forty years ago the Precisionist idea, in the painting of Georgia O'Keeffe, Charles Sheeler, Charles Demuth, and Niles Spencer, made its unheralded debut as a pioneer direction in modern American art.

As so often happens in the history of art, a descriptive term has become sanctified by usage, and since the appearance of the paintings by these artists the word "Precisionist" (and its less satisfactory synonym "Immaculate") continues to be employed in critical writing about their work.[1] In spite of the remarkable consistency in both their choice of subject and formal approach, the artists associated with the Precisionist direction, the personnel of which was in constant flux, never formed a "school," although in the Twenties many of them did show together under the auspices of a common gallery or in large, general exhibitions. Nor were there Precisionist manifestoes, publications, or programs of any sort. The earliest presentation of their pictures was primarily by a few adventurous and dedicated American dealers — Alfred Stieglitz, Charles Daniel, Stephan Bourgeois — who saw these paintings exclusively in terms of the ideals advanced by their own galleries. For example, Stieglitz, the most influential early champion of American painting, was con-

---

[1]*The exact origin of the terms Precisionist and Immaculate is vague. Henry McBride, the most prescient of American critics in the Twenties, said that "the Daniel Gallery, in the 1920's, began calling our attention to a group of clear-cut American painters who shortly became known as the Immaculates. . . ." ("An Elegant American Painter,"* Art News, *March, 1954, p. 21.) For such artists as Sheeler, O'Keeffe, and Ralston Crawford, the term has a pejorative connotation: like a Good Housekeeping seal of approval, says Sheeler. (Letter to M.F., April 26, 1960.)*

John I. H. Baur, in his exceptionally thorough book Revolution and Tradition in Modern American Art *(Cambridge, Harvard University Press, 1951), says, "The group of artists who fashioned the principal compromise between abstract principles and American realism are sometimes called the precisionists, sometimes the Immaculates. Both words are descriptive of their smooth, precise technique and their compositions of sharp-edged, simplified forms painted on large areas of unmodulated color." (P. 58.)*

In his perceptive essay "Cubist-Realism: An American Style" (Marsyas, Institute of Fine Arts, New York University, *Vol. III, 1946, pp. 139-60) and in his useful book* American Painting from the Armory Show to the Depression *(Princeton, N.J., Princeton University Press, 1955), Milton W. Brown deals with the styles of most of the painters considered here to be within the Precisionist context. His classificatory term "Cubist-Realism" stresses especially the European origins of the style.*

vinced that within his gallery alone the new American art spirit was being formed. Although he was well acquainted with the work of Sheeler and was an important sponsor of Demuth, for Stieglitz the ultimate American trinity was Georgia O'Keeffe, Arthur Dove, and John Marin.[2]

Charles Daniel has been described as America's least known hero of the arts. In addition to his early support of Marin, Hartley, Pascin, and Kuniyoshi, he presented the paintings of many of the Precisionists long before these artists had a substantial audience. Demuth exhibited with the Daniel Gallery beginning in 1913 and, a year later, had his first one-man show there; in 1922, Spencer joined the gallery, and that year he and Sheeler were given important one-man exhibitions. During the Twenties, Daniel also showed the work of Elsie Driggs and Peter Blume and continued encouragement of Preston Dickinson through his frequent periods of illness and emotional crisis.

At this time, George Ault and Stefan Hirsch were being presented by Bourgeois as the "Naives," the true successors of the earlier American primitives. "For the first time in its history," exclaimed Bourgeois in 1923, "America is on a sound foundation of thought. The future belongs to the Naive and the children."[3] Bourgeois construed these artists to be free from the weakening influences of Europe and, together with other painters in his gallery — Joseph Stella, Oscar Bluemner, Emile Branchard, Vincent Canadé, Maurice Sterne, and Arnold Friedman — they were to be the creators of a new American painting.

The Whitney Studio Club offered exhibitions and early support to such artists as Sheeler and Spencer during the Twenties. Other pioneer galleries included those of J. B. Neumann, who, during those years, initiated major exhibitions for Sheeler, Driggs, and Louis Lozowick. The Montross Gallery and Rehn Gallery also showed Precisionist paintings, and in 1926 Edith Gregor Halpert established The Downtown Gallery, whose activities still represent the most significant extension of the earlier exhibition programs. Today the localized boundaries of gallery loyalties that existed in the Twenties seem less urgent and it is clear now that we are dealing with a much broader, pervasive idea whose inspiration was in the air of that time.

*   *   *

Photographically realistic or abstract, the art of the Precisionists — whether a Sheeler industrial scene or an O'Keeffe portrait of an old Taos church — reflects an idealized state of absolute order. Time and space are not particularized and shadows cast by buildings are more important as elements of the picture's composition than as clues to the time of day. Light quality, even from a nonspecific source, is brilliant, never vague or "atmospheric," and forms on the horizon are handled as sharply as major elements in the foreground. The hour and season are lost, even in the most objectively rendered paintings by Sheeler, O'Keeffe, Blume, and Guglielmi.

The Precisionist painting process is one of continual editing. The pictures are brought to an icily defined and flawless finish, with virtually no evidence of the brush strokes or the trials and hesitations of arriving at the finished stage. In its complete subordination of the medium, there is little reveling in the sensuous qualities of pigment, and the process of painting is skillfully buried under the polished surface. On this point, Sheeler states the Precisionist attitude: "I just don't want to see any more than is absolutely necessary of the physical materials that go into a picture."[4]

The Precisionist approach is dominated by the studio; it is an analytical still-life tradition that retains its hermetic quality even when taken outdoors. Standard studio arrangements of flowers and fruit, or buildings seen from the studio window are treated with equal impersonality. The vitality of this painting is in its insistent logic and discipline, through which the familiar object — a building, a complex machine, or even a flower — is stripped to its ultimate structure and presented with astonishing lucidity.

Neither impulse nor spontaneity plays a part in the development of elements in Precisionist paintings. Yet both the deliberate and unconscious retention of past events generates both the most literal and most abstract of the Precisionist images. Peter Blume described "a curious process or alchemy by which a number of diverse ideas out of the accumulation of images and experiences are suddenly brought together into a unified picture."[5] Crawford's repertoire of remembered images has become so distilled that similar shapes reappear constantly in new geographical contexts. The most traveled of the Precisionists, he takes his environment with him, carefully filtering the forms and colors of each new scene.

*　　　*　　　*

---

[2]In an important volume of essays dedicated to Stieglitz, Ralph Flint described "the final resolution of the Stieglitz idea as embodied in the work of Marin, O'Keeffe, and Dove, the three Americans who round out a full picture of his artistic credo." (America and Alfred Stieglitz, Waldo Frank, et al., eds., Garden City, N. Y., Doubleday, Doran and Co., Inc., 1934, p. 176.) And yet, for all jealous partisanship of these three, Stieglitz, in Edna Bryner's fervent words, "sustained by uncanny knowing could let an artist, a Marin, an O'Keeffe, a Dove, be himself, herself, and himself again and again times over in the open eyes of everyone: . . ." (Ibid., p. 256.)

[3]Annual Exhibition of American Painters and Sculptors, New York, Bourgeois Galleries, Inc., 1923. Bourgeois has a curiously personal definition of "Naive," equating it with "imagination."

[4]Conversation with M.F., June 18, 1959.

[5]Quoted by James Thrall Soby in "Peter Blume's Eternal City," Museum of Modern Art Bulletin (New York), April, 1943, p. 6.

Through all the arrivals and departures of the painters within the Precisionist context, O'Keeffe and Sheeler, working independently and in increasing isolation, have come to represent the two main currents of Precisionist expression.[6] Extreme simplification of form, unwavering, sharp delineation, and carefully reasoned abstract organization are the stylistic qualities most conspicuously common to the work of both. And still, within the Precisionist microcosm their painting could be described as the traditional romantic-classic duality. For the most part, O'Keeffe's images of a monumentalized natural world are concerned with the primal forces of creation and decay. In contrast, Sheeler's architectural and mechanical subjects are chaste celebrations of the more immediate and tangible spirit of modern technology.

The styles of both have fluctuated between abstraction and photographic realism, but O'Keeffe has always been much more interested in completely non-figurative painting. Beginning with the interpretive drawings that first attracted Stieglitz in 1916, she was to evolve an organic, abstract style whose inspiration was in the desolate landscapes of Texas and New Mexico. At the same time that she was producing the paintings of flowers, bones, and barns for which she is best known, she carried her anatomical form of non-figurative art into the mid-Twenties in such works as "Dark Abstraction," 1924, and "Abstraction,"* 1926.

The influence of photography has been substantial in the work of both O'Keeffe and Sheeler. After completing his training at the Pennsylvania Academy of the Fine Arts, Sheeler set himself up in business as an architectural photographer. On moving to New York in 1919, he widened his activity to include photographing art objects for galleries and working with Edward Steichen on Vogue magazine. Although he always considered himself first a painter, Sheeler's New York exhibition in 1920 at the De Zayas Gallery included photographs of industrial sites and African sculpture as well as paintings, and that year he cooperated with Paul Strand in making a spectacular film essay, Manahatta, which was one of the first to communicate the strength, scale, and impressive geometry of the modern metropolis. A major commission came in 1927 when the Ford Motor Company asked him to photograph the buildings, machinery, and manufacturing processes of its River Rouge plant.

The dynamics of cinematic photography, with all its new visual possibilities — dramatic perspective and the contrasting of panorama and detail, for example — had a lasting effect on Sheeler's painting. Significantly, these aspects of the camera were of more interest to him then than its reportorial uses.[7] With the exception of such specialized projects as his Chartres Cathedral series of 1929 and the series of Assyrian reliefs commissioned by the Metropolitan Museum in 1942, his approach to photography has been one of selective vision — and, as in his painting, it has been the industrial subject that has most strongly moved him.

O'Keeffe, through her association with the Stieglitz group, encountered a still more experimental attitude toward photography. This was an entirely revolutionary philosophy about the lyric possibilities of the camera, an emphasis on psychological qualities revealable by new techniques. It was a rejection of the picturesque, salon approach that Stieglitz, with great effectiveness, railed against throughout his career. Edward Steichen and Paul Strand, both influenced and encouraged by Stieglitz, used in their work many of the devices that characterize O'Keeffe's painting: the sudden enlargement of an architectural detail, the close-range, intimate view of a flower section which, while all outside contours and references disappear, reveals an unsuspected, new identity.[8] Stieglitz's own photographs of New York perhaps had less effect on O'Keeffe's painting than might be imagined. On the contrary, as Doris Bry suggests, Stieglitz in his more experimental photography may have been strongly influenced by O'Keeffe's style.[9]

---

[6]*Curiously, O'Keeffe never had any direct disciples, although the woods were full of pallid imitators. This was not the case with Sheeler, whose painting was germinal to the work of many of the other artists included in this exhibition.*

Asterisks indicate illustrated works.

[7]*But Sheeler has always maintained a distinction between his painting and photography. Referring to the inevitable comparisons between his performances in each medium, he says the redisposition of visual elements is the prerogative of the painter. "Yet photography by its limitations is confined to presentation of an image without the arbitrary redisposal of elements within the total image." Quoted by George M. Craven in "Sheeler at Seventy-Five,"* College Art Journal, *Winter, 1959, p. 138.*

[8]*Harold Clurman's perceptive comment on Strand's photographic technique readily applies to O'Keeffe's celebrated flower pictures. Here are familiar objects "too far aloof to lend themselves to our needs or to yield to the pressure of our desires. They are they; forever and ever immutable, solitary, inexorable and magnificent." ("Photographs by Paul Strand,"* Creative Art, *October, 1929, pp. 735-38.)*

[9]*"Alfred Stieglitz: Photographer,"* Exhibition of Photographs by Alfred Stieglitz, *National Gallery of Art, Washington, D.C., 1958.*

EARLY ECHOES OF EUROPE

Sheeler   LANDSCAPE, 1915   William H. Lane Foundation

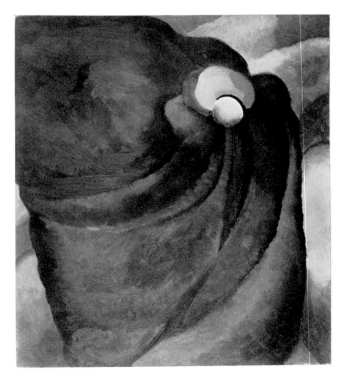

O'Keeffe   LAKE GEORGE, COAT AND RED, 1919

The Downtown Gallery

Demuth WHITE ARCHITECTURE, 1917 William H. Lane Foundation

VARIATIONS ON THE CUBIST IDEA

Sheeler   AMERICANA, 1931   Mr. and Mrs. Milton Lowenthal

Crawford   THIRD AVENUE EL, 1949   Walker Art Center

Demuth   STAIRS, PROVINCETOWN, 1920   Museum of Modern Art

Spencer   CITY WALLS, 1921   Museum of Modern Art

MEASURED RURAL ARCHITECTURE

O'Keeffe   LAKE GEORGE BARNS, 1926   Walker Art Center

O'Keeffe   STABLES, 1932   Detroit Institute of Arts

Sheeler BUCKS COUNTY BARN, 1923   Whitney Museum of American Art

Sheeler ON A SHAKER THEME, 1956   Mr. and Mrs. Stephen A. Stone

TRADITIONS, INFLUENCES, AND PARALLELS

The Precisionist movement is an extension of an objective and literal native American style. The homage it pays to utilitarian objects and the surroundings of daily life relates it to the sober homilies of the American primitive painters. Sheeler's barns and Shaker farmhouse interiors and Demuth's colonial churches and Pennsylvania cotton mills are themselves tributes to this earlier native tradition. Many of the American scene paintings of Sheeler, Dickinson, Spencer, and Demuth could even be considered extreme forms of regionalism. But if many Precisionists practiced a descriptive art, their paintings did not share the regionalists' anecdotal basis; the "pure" regionalist attitude, evident in the work of John Steuart Curry, Grant Wood, and Thomas Benton in the Thirties, was loudly evangelical and chauvinistic.[10]

The Precisionist direction must also be considered as a conscious if often elementary attempt to harmonize the earlier American visual tradition with random elements from the exploding nebulae of modern European art.

Cubism (and to a lesser extent its offspring Futurism, Constructivism, and Orphism) was the most powerful of the European influences to be felt by the Precisionists, and its effects still pervade their most recent work. Of the original group, Demuth, Sheeler, Spencer, and Dickinson independently visited or worked in Paris[11] but began to use Cubism only after Picasso and Braque had abandoned its purely analytical form in 1914; their inheritance was a miscellany of floating elements — the already hardening forms of a brilliant, short-lived style.

The Precisionists were not so much innovators or theorists as they were synthesizers. Unlike their contemporaries in Holland, Germany, and Russia who were evolving sub-schools that carried Cubist philosophy into new directions and applications, the Precisionists had less interest in Cubism's abstruse ideology than in the pragmatic use of its forms and formulae. Well before the full emergence of the Precisionist attitude as such in the Twenties, these artists were experimenting with Cubism, yet, with the notable exception of Demuth, none of this group seems to have been concerned with assimilating the metaphysics of the French style. The techniques of Cubism, without reference to its frequently arcane doctrines, seemed particularly suited to the subjects of the young Precisionists, who, revolting against the turgid "Munichoiserie"[12] of their early training, were now turning for their themes to the nation's phenomenally growing cities and industry. Here were ready-made "cubistic" forms — skyscrapers, bridges, docks, grain elevators, turbines, cranes — and through Precisionist painting these became the dominant images in American art.

Excellent examples of Cubism's early influence on the Precisionist direction are found in the work of Charles Demuth. A thoroughly sophisticated spirit, he was intrigued by the Cubists' subtle dissolution and regeneration of form. His mastery of the Cubist rule book is clearly evident in his earliest works that may be called Precisionist, a group of watercolor improvisations on building themes executed in 1917. In the same year he painted "White Architecture,"* a picture that contains all the essentials of analytical Cubism. Here color is used sparingly to modify a complex of intersecting planes, buildings reduced to anonymity in typical Cubist style, and the emphasis is on fragile angularity and decorous surface. Interestingly, the fugal, Gothic feeling of the painting recalls the work of Feininger, who, in Germany, even earlier was applying Cubist methodology in his spiritualized paintings of buildings.

Although Sheeler had visited Europe earlier, his real introduction to Cubism came through the Armory Show in 1913.[13] Impressed by the exhibition's brilliant French section, he began painting Cubist-inspired pictures of the barns and landscape around Doylestown, Pennsylvania.[14] These early pictures are vigorous arabesques of buildings, trees, sky, and ground, and already, as in "Landscape,"* 1915, Sheeler's interest in the architectural subject is stated. In this early picture, in spite of its free brushing, there is a careful underlying plan that marks his adoption of Cubist techniques. By 1919, Sheeler had drastically disciplined his brushwork, sharpened the contours of his forms, and was producing still more austere Cubist landscapes and still lifes.

---

[10]*Wood borrowed a concise, North European rendering technique and replaced fifteenth-century Flanders with a prettified Iowa. Yet some of his portraits and whimsical interpretations of American history come close to Precisionist clarity and feeling.*

[11]*Sheeler as a student at the Pennsylvania Academy of the Fine Arts accompanied William Merritt Chase's classes on summer trips to Europe, beginning in 1904. Demuth in 1907 was in Paris during the first days of Cubism. Dickinson went to Europe in 1910. Spencer made his first visit to France and Italy in 1921. O'Keeffe did not go abroad until 1953 but of course had excellent opportunity to see products of current European art movements in Stieglitz's galleries.*

[12]*During the 1870's, Munich was Mecca for the generation that was to teach the Precisionists. Chase transmuted the sober Munich style into a dashing technique of facile brushwork and glittering surfaces. That ebullient master taught at the Art Student's League in New York and in Philadelphia at the Pennsylvania Academy of the Fine Arts, and among his many students were Sheeler, Schamberg, Demuth, and O'Keeffe. Their reactions to the methods he advanced are arresting. Leaving the League in 1908, O'Keeffe, though a star performer in Chase's class, considered giving up serious painting and worked a year in Chicago as an advertising artist. While he considered Chase an inspiring teacher, Sheeler feels his recovery required even longer. After he left the Academy in 1906, he states, "It took me ten years to bail out." (Conversation with M.F., June 18, 1959.)*

[13]*Sheeler, at this point greatly interested in Cézanne's structural approach, was invited by Arthur B. Davies to submit six works to the Armory show; Sheeler's friend Schamberg was also represented by a group of paintings, chiefly landscapes with arbitrary color.*

[14]*Sheeler rented a simple eighteenth-century farmhouse near Doylestown for weekends of painting while working as an architectural photographer in Philadelphia. From about 1913 up until Schamberg's death in 1918, Sheeler and his friend wandered around this Pennsylvania Dutch region sketching, acquiring pottery and furniture, and studying the local collections of early American furniture and crafts.*

The clinical vision of Cubism reached even O'Keeffe — seemingly the most removed from its influence — in her most literal paintings of desert bones, shells, and flowers. The forceful color spirals of "Lake George, Coat and Red,"* 1919, recall the Orphist or Synchromist approaches of Delaunay or MacDonald-Wright,[15] and her paintings of architectural themes, whether the New York skyscraper series or, especially, her more recent Abiquiu "patio" group of the mid-Fifties, treat the planes of these structures with characteristic Cubist economy.

Preston Dickinson, living in Europe from 1910 to 1915, had first-hand acquaintance with nascent Cubist characteristics. His paintings after that period have much in common with Cubism's "primitive" phase, especially the 1908 L'Estaque landscapes of Braque, which systematically brutalized picturesque subject matter in penetrating to the essence of structure. And, like the Cubists, Dickinson found a precedent for this handling in the later Cézanne landscapes. By 1919, Dickinson was producing a series of watercolors and drawings of houses and mountains whose origins were unmistakably in Cézanne's Mont St. Victoire pictures. In these paintings the forms are flattened, layeredup in shallow space, and the complexes of rugged topography and jagged roof lines result in vigorous, aggressive patterns.

Two other important European movements, Dada and Surrealism, paralleled the evolution of the Precisionist approach. While the major European influence came from Cubism, the pioneer Precisionists were well aware of Dada and Surrealist activity. Picabia in 1913 had his first American exhibition at "291." Marcel Duchamp, who in 1912 participated in the first Futurist exhibition held in Paris, came to New York in 1915 and the next year promoted the revolutionary spirit of Dada — an interest in the "commonplace," not the beautiful. Stieglitz's magazine 291 was publishing critiques of the Dada work of Picabia, De Zayas, Picasso, and Apollinaire. The 67th Street house of the poet and art collector Walter Arensberg was turned into an all-night salon and showcase for international Dadaism where Duchamp and Picabia, as practically permanent guests, expounded Dada's nihilistic disdain for sacred traditions. Sheeler and Demuth were among the many American painters present.[16]

The effect of Dada was especially apparent in the witty paintings of Sheeler's close friend Morton Schamberg. Both young men were interested in painting the machine. For Sheeler, its geometric forms and inhuman efficiency made it an admirable subject for painting that was to be "engineered." But Schamberg (whose most serious involvement was actually in Cubism and its techniques), in the cynical spirit of Dada, took a less sober view. As in "Telephone," 1916, he slyly mocked the modern artifacts which in their astonishing

Demuth   MY EGYPT, 1927   Whitney Museum of American Art

O'Keeffe   NEW YORK NIGHT, 1929   Nebraska Art Association

Spencer   WAKE OF THE HURRICANE, 1951   Walker Art Center

ubiquity had taken on an uncomfortably human quality. In his paintings, the shapes of these everyday mechanical wonders were dissected and regrouped into whimsical arrangements. But his art went beyond satire and, in the review of Schamberg's memorial exhibition at Knoedler's in the spring of 1919, one critic, possibly McBride, wrote in the New York Sun, "It seems absurd to say that Schamberg has evolved structures as beautiful as flowers from machine forms and yet there is no other way to express the fact that beauty is the result."

The spirit of Dada also lurked in Demuth's transmutations of his Pennsylvania subjects. While Sheeler's industrial paintings have been described as proud visions seen from the eye of management, Demuth's paintings of the same structures suggest a cultivated eighteenth-century mentality regarding with amusement and refined disdain the systematic obliteration of its epoch. He had only to look out the window of his Lancaster house at the local skyline with its anachronistic counterpoint of colonial church, nineteenth-century cotton mill, and twentieth-century grain elevators, smokestacks, and water-towers. These were his subjects, and he titled them cryptically and amusingly. The imposing grain elevators of John W. Eshelman and Sons, dominating the brick and clapboard structures of an older Lancaster, looked to him like a vision of Karnak; they became "My Egypt,"* 1927. Change was not equated with progress for Demuth, and "After All...,"* 1933, is a comment on the monstrous appurtenances of modern industry pushing the venerable town out of the century.

Surrealist philosophy could not have been more opposite to that of the Precisionists, yet it had its parallels to and effects upon the work of a number of them. As proclaimed by André Breton in 1924, Surrealism was a flight from the world of appearances to the reality of "the marvelous" through the antique and the world of dreams; Sheeler's glorified vision of a brave new world of technology was the very thing the Surrealists rejected.[17] And the seemingly

---

[15]*In 1917, Stieglitz arranged the first American one-man exhibition of S. MacDonald-Wright's painting at "291."*

[16]*Others of the European contingent were Gleizes and Crotti, and among the Americans were also Joseph Stella, Marsden Hartley, Isadora Duncan, Katherine Dreier, Amy Lowell, and William Carlos Williams. The house throbbed with genial confusion loudly punctuated by battles and intrigues as the perpetual guests assailed each other's positions. In 1922, the exhausted Arensbergs fled to California, collection and all.*

[17]*The one occasion on which Sheeler painted a picture that might superficially be considered Surrealist was in 1943, when in* The Artist Looks at Nature *(not in the exhibition) he depicted himself, back to the viewer, sitting at work before his easel. The landscape surrounding him, however, is more in the spirit of a Flemish pastorale, tidy and distinct. Sheeler considers this work a sport, inconsistent with his development and his one attempt in the direction of metaphysics. (Conversation with M.F., June 18, 1959.)*

undisciplined aspects of Surrealism — the automatic writing of Masson, for example, the unmapped venture into the unknown — were completely absent in Precisionist art. Yet, disregarding Surrealism's almost pathological negativism — and this is hard to do — it is still true that the hyper-reality of the "hand-painted dreams" of Ernst, Tanguy, Dali, and Roy was then the most significant development in a new, international literalism.[18]

Blume's "White Factory," 1928, for example, uses the Surrealist device of paradox: a clutter of old, weathered buildings contrast with the doorless and windowless structure of the "factory" so generalized in its shining representation that its exact function can never be guessed. Yet the use of such devices on Blume's part never stemmed from the desire merely to shock. And even at this period of parallels to Surrealism (as well as to Sheeler's work), Blume's deeper affinities were with the thirteenth- and fourteenth-century Italian primitives. By the time Blume went to Italy, in 1932, the Precisionist direction, with its fundamental impersonality, had almost completely lost its meaning for him. His art increasingly took its elements from allegory and archaeology. Alternately biting and compassionate, his work continues to dwell on the follies of modern man.

Guglielmi used a Surrealist vocabulary to describe the loneliness of city life, as in "A Muted Street,"* 1942, with its isolated figures and subtly distorted bridge and buildings. But unlike the Surrealists he was genuinely concerned with the immediate, human situation. A young Italian immigrant, Guglielmi had lived with his family in the slums of East Harlem and had seen transplanted to the tenement districts of New York the customs, rituals, and superstitions of the impoverished Italian village — in itself a somewhat Surrealist experience. "At that time it was a poor section of foreign born, a veritable jungle that delighted and frightened me, and which I also rejected."[19] As neon lights gradually replaced the candles of the religious festival, the symbols of technology became to Guglielmi the symbols of hope, and his art aspired to "give the people a reason to live out the debris of our years."[20] As Crawford was to carry the geometric aspects of Precisionist painting to new limits, linking it to the development of American abstract art in the Forties, Guglielmi almost a decade earlier represented a transition between the Precisionists and the social realists.

Certainly O'Keeffe's rose-bedecked animal skulls floating over the desert recall the Surrealist device of using unexpected combinations of familiar objects in vistas of desolation. But the symbolism in O'Keeffe's painting has more in common with the impersonal asceticism of Oriental art and the spiritualized visions of Odilon Redon than with Surrealism.[21] The strength of her images is in their simplicity and their power to evoke the history and environment from which they have been clinically isolated. A self-conscious art criticism of the Twenties, however, fashioned a writing about her painting that found its metaphors in the new Freudian thinking. Most of these speculations were inspired by her well known flower paintings, with their fantastic monumentalizing of mysterious inner botanical structures. "Well — I made you take time to look at what I saw and when you took time to really notice my flower you hung all your own associations with flowers on my flower and you write about my flower as if I think and see what you think and see of the flower — and I don't."[22] This accusation still stands as Georgia O'Keeffe's answer to the generations of American art critics for whom a favorite, chronic indulgence has been the relentless search for hidden meanings, erotic meaning particularly, in her art.

In 1936, the critics were still trying to fathom her intentions. "What does she mean?" wrote Henry McBride. "The bleached skull with the rampant horns is beautiful. Is death, then beautiful?"[23] Lewis Mumford associated these pictures with O'Keeffe's serious illness prior to their production.[24] But she regained her health and resumed her remarkable output, still not bothering to explain her grim themes. (Marsden Hartley had commented earlier on her durability when he wrote, "She looks as if she had ridden the million miles of her every known horizon, and has left all her horses lying dead in their tracks."[25]) O'Keeffe, in spite of the esoteric symbolism of these paintings, had no acquaintance with Surrealist personalities and less interest in their credos.

---

[18]*In Germany, equivalents in technique were found in the cynical Neue Sachlikeit of Otto Dix and George Grosz. The work of Pierre Roy, in France, is perhaps closest to the sharp objectivity of Sheeler; an accomplished technician, Roy is the only Surrealist for whose work Sheeler expresses admiration. (Conversation with M.F., June 19, 1959.)*

[19]*O. Louis Guglielmi, "I Hope to Sing Again,"* Magazine of Art, *May, 1944, p. 175.*

[20]*Quoted in* American Realists and Magic Realists *(Dorothy Miller and Alfred H. Barr, Jr., eds.), Museum of Modern Art, New York, 1943, p. 39.*

[21]*O'Keeffe's interest in Oriental art has continued since her studies with Arthur Wesley Dow at Columbia Teachers College in 1914. Dow, who had been a disciple of the noted Orientalist Ernest F. Fenellosa in 1889, was in 1887 one of the group of young painters with Gauguin at Pont Aven. In Dow's classes, students made imaginative interpretations based on the forms and colors of Persian ceramics, Chinese painting, etc. The result of Dow's teaching process was the evolution of a system of flat, patterned, linear forms. His teaching techniques revolutionized American art education, but in the hands of less imaginative students, Dow's methods — still in existence, surprisingly — have long since become stifling and pedantic.*

[22]*Georgia O'Keeffe, "About Myself,"* Exhibition of Oils and Pastels, *An American Place, New York, 1939.*

[23]New York Sun, *January 13, 1936.*

[24]*"Autobiographies in Paint,"* The New Yorker, *January 18, 1936, p. 48.*

[25]Adventures in the Arts, *New York, Boni and Liveright, 1921, p. 117.*

THE URBAN THEMES

In the Twenties the Precisionist thesis became as crystallized as the surfaces of its paintings. The formative influences, particularly Cubism, had been as much absorbed as they were ever to be. And during this time the Precisionists made their most impressive contribution. The forms and techniques they had been refining for the previous five to ten years found application in a singularly appropriate subject which, in turn, reinforced their procedure. Indeed, if there is a unifying characteristic of Precisionist painting, it is the attraction of all its artists to the colossal geometry of the city and industry.

In the Precisionist paintings of skyscrapers, bridges, factories, and docks, all traces of damage or decay disappeared, specific architectural details were vastly simplified, and these forms were recast as the proud symbols of technological splendor. The first city paintings of Sheeler, for example, like the earlier, more expressionistic idealizations of Joseph Stella, combined a sense of awe with a commitment to the idea of progress. The Precisionist visions of the metropolis present a hard-edged, invincible Utopia. In these paintings the crenelated New York skyline, the city's patterns of high speed traffic, the busy harbors — in short, all the ingredients that have figured in every subsequent visual cliché about the city — were used for the first time with vigor and originality.

In the earliest Sheeler painting or the most recent Crawford, there has been no apparent involvement with the serious sociological issues attending the technological transformation of this country. The almost total absence of the human figure in Precisionist images of the man-made world is in itself an implicit rejection of such immediate issues. While America was living through the frenetic Twenties and the doleful years of the Depression, O'Keeffe and Sheeler — nearly all the Precisionist painters, in fact — refused to let this disquiet permeate the idealized world of their art. Nor did the Precisionist development argue for a cause, a continual source of irritation to those critics who want their painting well laced with message.[26] Guglielmi and Blume were the notable exceptions in their morality plays staged within the structures of the indifferent city.

It was during the Twenties, because of their avid interest in the city as a subject, that the Precisionists seemed most nearly a group. "The Men," as O'Keeffe refers to the painters and photographers of the Stieglitz circle — Marin, Weber, Steichen, Strand, and Stieglitz himself — while producing their own interpretive portraits of the metropolis, were amused that even she would want to depart from her familiar repertory of flowers, rocks, and barns to paint the buildings of New York.

Through the windows of Stieglitz's "Intimate Gallery" and from the heights of her Shelton Hotel apartment overlooking the East River the patterns and vitality of the city seemed to O'Keeffe to reflect the same kind of organic evolution that so interested her in nature. She painted these subjects for only a limited period, between 1926 and 1929 when she produced the eloquent series that includes "New York Night,"* 1929. In the city paintings, O'Keeffe's approach is curiously impressionistic: the typical Precisionist sharp contours are present but the real emphasis is on the opulent surface decoration, a patterning in which volume is dissolved. There is actually a greater sense of architectural structure in such paintings as her Taos canvases of the Ranchos Church begun in 1929, works which immediately followed her New York sky-scraper series.

Within the limits of the urban-oriented Precisionist iconography, there are major differences of emphasis. Sheeler, who has never veered from the pristine architectural style he developed to its fullest in the Twenties, was the strongest and most consistent in his objective exploitation of the city themes, and undoubtedly he exerted considerable influence on many of the younger painters such as Blume, Hirsch, Driggs, and Lozowick who were working in this vein.

Spencer, whose admiration for Sheeler's painting was unqualified, was ex-clusively interested in the city as a source of structural relationships, and, as such, he never idealized the subject. His painting is rougher than Sheeler's and its surfaces and contours consciously avoid finality. "City Walls,"* 1921, more than any other painting, foreshadowed the important abstract develop-ment in Spencer's work of twenty years later. Of the early Precisionists, it was Spencer whose work most persistently and conspicuously retained the techniques of Cubism, particularly in his adherence to low-key color.

If many of the younger painters took Sheeler's model for their urban paint-ings, it would be wrong to assume that each shared his disciplined objectivity. Within the so quickly codified Precisionist themes and techniques, there existed, even in the early phase of the movement, a variety of attitudes which ranged from Lozowick's fanciful glorifications of the American city to Ault's abhorrence of the "dark, dank caverns" of its streets.

---

[26]*An extreme though not particularly surprising reaction was registered by Charles Cor-win in the* New York Daily Worker *on February 4, 1949: "Sheeler approaches the in-dustrial landscape, whether it be farm buildings, textile mills or oil refineries with the same sort of piety Fra Angelico used toward angels. His architecture remains pure and uncontaminated with any trace of humans or human activity, an industrialist's heaven where factories work themselves. In revealing the beauty of factory architecture, Sheeler has become the Raphael of the Fords. Who is it that will be the Giotto of the U.A.W.?"*

Ault   SULLIVAN STREET ABSTRACTION, 1928   Zabriskie Gallery

Sheeler   MANCHESTER, 1949   Baltimore Museum of Art

Hirsch   NEW YORK, LOWER MANHATTAN, 1921   The Phillips Collection

THREE VIEWS OF THE BRIDGE

Blume   THE BRIDGE, 1928   Mr. and Mrs. Martin Janis

Guglielmi A MUTED STREET, 1942 Mrs. Edith Gregor Halpert

Lozowick NEW YORK, 1926-27 Lent by the artist

Between 1926 and 1927, Lozowick produced an impressive series of American city canvases. Through conventionalized references, he wanted to show the force and character of "the skyscrapers of New York, the grain elevators of Minneapolis, the steel mills of Pittsburgh, the oil wells of Oklahoma, the copper mines of Butte, the lumber yards of Seattle." He summed up his feeling about his subjects when he wrote in a statement for the catalogue of the "Machine Age Exposition" in 1927 that "beneath all the apparent chaos and confusion," America was moving toward "order and organization which find their outward sign and symbol in the rigid geometry of the American city: in the verticals of its smoke stacks, in the parallels of its car tracks, the squares of its streets, the cubes of its factories, the arc of its bridges, the cylinders of its gas tanks." Using this "underlying mathematical pattern," the perceptive artist could create a new expression of optimism, and "In this manner the flowing rhythm of modern America may be gripped and stayed and its synthesis eloquently rendered in the native idiom."[27]

Lozowick took apart and reassembled the salient elements of each city he represented. Of his painting "New York,"* 1926-27, he writes that after many preliminary studies, "the bridges, the elevated lines, the skyscrapers were manipulated in various combinations"[28] to reach a satisfactory solution. The quality of these paintings is remarkably close to the Futurist dynamism of Stella and the spirit of the European Constructivists. This is not entirely surprising, for Lozowick since 1921 had been periodically visiting France and Germany, and in 1922 his "mechanistic" paintings were included in the First International Exhibition held in Düsseldorf. There he found himself in the company of such artists as Gabo, van Doesburg, Moholy-Nagy, and El Lissitsky. Interestingly, his first works shown in Europe were widely interpreted as true expressions of America.[29]

In his painting "New York, Lower Manhattan,"* 1921, Stefan Hirsch seemed to share Lozowick's optimism about the city. The elegant complex of perfectly ordered, flattened building blocks prompted Stephan Bourgeois to write, "Here we have not so much an actual portrait of the City as it looks, but an image of its motive-power — indeed a city of terrific mental activity."[30] Yet this sonorous description did not reflect Hirsch's attitudes as he recalls them, and the idealized calm of "New York, Lower Manhattan" is strangely at variance with Hirsch's stated feelings about the city. Returning to New York from a long sojourn in Europe after World War I, he said that "instead of finding the fresh, open view which I had idealistically assumed to exist from reading Walt Whitman, Emerson and Thoreau, I was confronted with the piles of steel and concrete that keep all the sun from the Wall Street area." The window-lessness of this painting's buildings was "not altogether the accident of abstraction but also expressed my recoil from the monstrosity that industrial life had become in 'megapolitania.' "[31]

Within the rigidity of the Precisionist style there were strongly dissonant, introspective elements. Although clearly influenced by Sheeler's concept of the city, much of Ault's work has a peculiarly haunted quality, and his total production remained remarkably unresolved.[32] For a time he made sallies into Surrealism and painted Breughelesque landscapes around Woodstock. His work patterns were erratic and he was a victim of his own virtuosity and emotionality. Life in New York became intolerable for him: this city was "the inferno without the fire." These feelings are perhaps best expressed in the melancholy "Sullivan Street Abstraction,"* 1928, whose buildings are faceless as they swiftly recede to a constellation of lights suspended from no visible source. Yet, three years before his death in 1948, Ault was to return to this same image, virtually repainting it without change.[33]

The metamorphosis of the city was accompanied by an even more spectacular alteration in the spirit and substance of industry, and during the Twenties America witnessed the accelerated introduction of mechanization through assembly lines, mass production, and enormous industrial plants within and outside the city. New time- and labor-saving machinery of ingenious design appeared for every conceivable manufacturing process. Even the fear of what the machine might do to future employment was offset by the adulation in

---

[27]Louis Lozowick, "The Americanization of Art," Machine Age Exposition (sponsored by the Little Review and others), New York, 1927, pp. 18-19.

[28]Letter to M.F., March 16, 1960.

[29]This exhibition was more or less duplicated by the 1926 Société Anonyme-organized show at The Brooklyn Museum, "International Exhibition of Modern Art"; this included major figures in European abstraction and such Stieglitz-sponsored Americans as Marin, Hartley, Dove, Weber, and also, notably, O'Keeffe, Demuth, Spencer, Dickinson, and Lozowick.

[30]A Catalogue of Paintings by Stefan Hirsch, Bourgeois Galleries, Inc., New York, 1927.

[31]Letter to M.F., March 29, 1960.

[32]Perhaps one reason for this lack of resolution is discoverable in a comment by Lloyd Goodrich, whose review for The Arts (June, 1926, p. 347) of Ault's exhibition at the Neumann Galleries was generally favorable. But Goodrich could see the dangers of "a method like this, for the very qualities that give the work distinction may easily degenerate into mannerisms. In looking at some of the pictures one felt that there was a possibility that the tight painting, the brittle surfaces, the sharp-edged flat planes fitting one into another, may become a sort of intellectual game with the artist, taking the place of the deeper qualities of feeling and observation."

[33]His painting New Moon: New York, 1945 (not in the exhibition), was compositionally a complete return to Sullivan Street Abstraction except that skyscrapers, "tombstones of capitalism" as he termed them, were substituted for the smaller buildings of the earlier picture.

which it was held. While such Europeans as Duchamp and Picabia could at times regard the machine with jaundiced wit and disrespect, most of the Precisionists admired its forms and efficiency. Stella, a Futurist and our major link with the European tradition of the time, painted the industrial subject with extraordinary rapture. He wanted to convey its strength and audacious force, and the violently segmented, intersecting forms of his paintings were "an echo of the oceanic polyphony (never heard before) expressed by the steely orchestra of modern constructions." His purpose was to use all his "fire to forge . . . a gigantic art . . . far removed from the insignificant frivolities of easel pictures. . . ." It is interesting to note that although these were to proceed from "a mathematical precision of intent, animated only by essential elements,"[34] his industrial pictures have only a tangential relationship to the Precisionist development.

Thomas Hess, remarking on the Precisionists' "machine poetry," cited one of its peculiarities: the ability of a single artist to "alternate between magic realism and flat geometric abstraction."[35] There is no clearer evidence of this extraordinary stylistic range than a survey of the paintings of mechanical and industrial themes by Sheeler, "the good gray poet of American industry." The historic "Upper Deck," 1929, a photographically detailed study based on the steamship Majestic, was "the inauguration of a period that followed for a good many years: of planning a picture very completely before starting to work on the final canvas, having a blueprint of it and knowing just exactly what it was going to be. Not the accidental things, the touch of a brush that might be brilliant in its application, but having a basic plan."[36] This painting, aside from its importance in Sheeler's own development, can be considered the prototype for an extremely successful work by a younger man, Edmund Lewandowski. By the time Lewandowski painted his Great Lakes "Ore Freighter"* in 1948, an assured, meticulous view of a subject he knew well, Sheeler had already, almost ten years earlier, returned to a more abstract style. Through his painting of Milwaukee's docks and industries, Lewandowski, one of the most accomplished of the younger artists working in the Precisionist context during this period, had a significant role in extending the style into the Midwest.

In 1931 Sheeler painted "Classic Landscape," one of a group of pictures using the River Rouge sites he had photographed earlier in great detail. At this point his art had seemingly reached a plateau of objective realism. Still, it is a strongly idealized realism in which the simplified volumes of his architectural paintings of the early Twenties are given identity, often at the expense of the paintings' intrinsic abstract organization. "Classic Landscape," austere in its ordered cubes and cylinders, is for Sheeler the modern Arcadia. "Incantation,"* 1946, emphatically a return to his simpler abstract style, uses the enormous spheres and cylinders of a refinery's tanks and pipes to produce one of his most powerful commemorations of industry. Prior to the Forties, especially in his photographic paintings, color was a less important element, a tinting adjunct, but here it is used structurally to model the impressive volumes.

Sheeler's experience with photography continued to play a crucial role. "Aerial Gyrations," 1953, a study of a United States Steel blast furnace, illustrates an idea which had long occupied him, the retention and superimposition of a previous image as the basis for the process of abstraction. While Cubism and Surrealism in their separate ways carried this device to extremes, Sheeler used it as a photographer might employ a multiple exposure to convey the passage of time. Through these means, Sheeler advanced his increasingly personal abstract technique to its greatest elegance.

As in their city paintings, the Precisionist artists expressed a variety of responses to the phenomenon of industry. But, as noted earlier, none of their attitudes could be considered overtly critical — as were the reactions later, for example, of the social realists. Nor did all the Precisionists approach this subject from Sheeler's "engineering" point of view. For some, like Dickinson, the complex shapes of mechanization were lyricized into improbable, Jules Verne visions of industry: his arbitrarily faceted "Factory,"* 1924, has little to do with working units.

A similar attraction to the romance of the industrial subject distinguishes Elsie Driggs's 1927 painting of "Pittsburgh."* Wandering through the Jones and Laughlin steel mills, she was awed by their ominous beauty: "The particles of dust in the air seemed to catch and refract the light to make a backdrop of luminous pale gray behind the shapes of simple smoke stack and cone. To me it was Greek. What I went to see was a sight a Greco would have enjoyed painting. What I . . . painted when I returned was "Pittsburgh."[37] In this same style, Driggs painted a number of other Precisionist subjects: a River Rouge study, the Queensborough Bridge, a transport plane in flight. Unfortunately, these have disappeared through auctions and accidents and "Pittsburgh" now seems to be the only important surviving example of her early work.

By the end of the Twenties, the Precisionist idea had been completely stated and its future limits were thoroughly defined. However, for many young painters like Driggs the style was apparently too inhibiting and they cast about for

---

[34]*All quotes from Joseph Stella, "The Brooklyn Bridge (A Page of My Life),"* Transition *(Paris), Nos. 16 and 17, June, 1929, p. 36.*

[35]Art News, *November, 1947, p. 37.*

[36]*Conversation with M.F., June 18, 1959.*

[37]*Letter to M.F., March 23, 1960.* Pittsburgh *was immediately exhibited at Daniel's gallery, where it was hailed as the "New Classicism."*

REFLECTIONS OF AN INDUSTRIAL SOCIETY

Crawford   BOILER SYNTHESIS, 1942   Lent by the artist

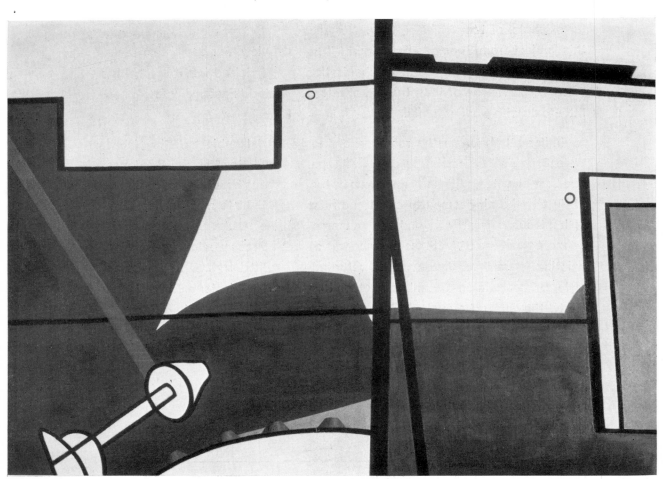

Sheeler   ROLLING POWER, 1939   Smith College Museum of Art

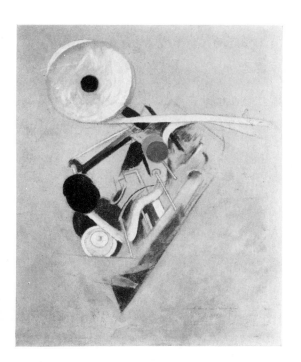

Schamberg   STILL LIFE, CAMERA FLASHLIGHT, 1916

Dr. and Mrs. Ira Leo Schamberg

Lewandowski   ORE FREIGHTER, 1948   Milwaukee Art Center

THE SOLID GEOMETRY OF INDUSTRY

Sheeler   INCANTATION, 1946   The Brooklyn Museum

Driggs   PITTSBURGH, 1927   Whitney Museum of American Art

Demuth   AFTER ALL ..., 1933

Norton Gallery and School of Art

Dickinson   FACTORY, 1924   Columbus Gallery of Fine Arts

new directions. What followed in the later work of the remaining group, especially Sheeler and O'Keeffe, was the elaboration, refinement — even the restatement — of the themes and techniques they evolved during that decade.

TOWARD LITERALISM

Although the Precisionist movement has shown little radical stylistic change since the Twenties, inevitably some fluctuations existed and, consistent with a general trend in American art, by the last half of the Twenties there was a perceptible shift toward literalism within the work of the whole group. Nevertheless, it was a qualified realism, involving neither a broadening nor a change of content, and its idealizing aspects prevailed over any strictly naturalistic tendencies. At all times the work of the major Precisionist artists remained an art of objects, formal rather than immediately expressive art, and — most important — the characteristic Precisionist sense of underlying structure was never lost.

These qualities were present in Sheeler's most meticulously detailed paintings during the Thirties of locomotives and power plants as well as of Shaker interiors and still lifes. Although Spencer's steel mill paintings and murals of the mid-decade might at first seem almost expressionistic in their loose forms and brushing, he never actually departed from his original, Cubist-oriented style. And O'Keeffe, too, who in 1929 began to spend much of her time in New Mexico, never ceased to reveal the inherent abstract structure in the desiccated souvenirs of her desert wanderings.

The emergence of heightened literalism can probably best be illustrated through a group of still life paintings. While still life painting was never a major preoccupation in Precisionist art, the choice of objects in the pictures that did appear, compared to the relatively inflexible forms of urban architecture, often makes these the most personal statements made by any of the artists in the movement.

Sheeler's "Americana,"* painted in 1931, reflects one of his greatest, lifelong interests: with utmost fidelity, he represented the Shaker furniture then in his South Salem, New York, house. Since his early painting excursions around the Doylestown countryside, Sheeler had been modestly acquiring important examples of early American furniture, rugs, and glass, and today his small house in Irvington-on-Hudson, converted from a gatekeeper's cottage, contains one of the best collections of folk art in the country.[38] These furnishings are in continuous and comfortable use (Sheeler even paints at a long, honey-colored Shaker table), and a visitor entering the house for the first time has the uncanny sensation that he is actually walking into a Sheeler painting.

By the time Sheeler painted "Americana," his literal technique was thoroughly developed, but, more important, so were his attitudes about painting. Expressly avoiding sentimentalism, he wanted in his work the same honesty and directness he admired in the artfully fashioned furniture and houses of the early Americans. Thus the absolute simplicity of "Americana" exploits none of the picturesque possibilities of the subject and his concern was almost completely with the architectural aspect of the total composition. It is a paradox that with all his admiration for the simple, planar forms of the American subject, Sheeler represented these through the disciplines of Cubism. Henry McBride, an eloquent and informed apostle of the "Modernist" cause,[39] amused by American distrust of European art, was quick to note that "Americana" showed how a "Yankee painter can get away with cubism in a country that says cubism is against the law."[40]

If "Green Table," 1930, is a realistic and introspective departure from Niles Spencer's Cubist works of a decade earlier, it still shows his almost obsessive interest in pure structure. Something between the spirit of Cézanne's modified realism and Spencer's first Cubist experiments, the solid, weighty presence of the objects — bottle, glasses, and a Panama hat placed on a simple studio table — is of more consequence than the exact colors, textures, or nuances of their surfaces. Nothing is tentative or impressionistically suggested; there is no weightlessness, fragility, or inconclusiveness about these objects, dense and solid as the architectural interior that supports and frames them.

As Hilaire Hiler states, Spencer was interested only in "structure and relations rather than in symbols, propaganda, esoteric theories, drama or melodrama...."[41] A morose and troubled individual, Spencer increasingly avoided new situations in his personal life and in his art. And, as though to avoid disturbing new challenges, he evolved a careful formula, a set of rigid rules for painting, within which he developed his language of understatement. The uniformity of his color, his unvaried paint surface, and the simplicity of his forms are both the strength and limitation of Spencer's art.

Dickinson's still life painting, as contrasted with his more geometricized fac-

---

[28]*Spencer, Demuth, and Ault, too, surrounded themselves with similar objects.*

[39]*"Modernism" appears to have been the convenient catchall for every American art movement past "The Eight" and served as a synonym for Post-Impressionism, Cubism, Futurism, and Expressionism, which "burst upon the American public" after the Armory Show in 1913. Deploring Demuth's "incidental lapses into pure abstraction," Frank Jewett Mather suggested that "A Modernist does not wish to be understood and appreciated too quickly." (Frank Jewett Mather, Jr., et al.,* The American Spirit in Art, *New Haven, Yale University Press, 1927, p. 165.)*

[40]*Henry McBride,* New York Sun, *November 21, 1931.*

[41]*Letter to M.F., May 3, 1960.*

tory pictures, represents his art's greatest degree of realism. More than any other Precisionist painter except Demuth, Dickinson belonged to that remote, rarified climate of American art in the Twenties whose paintings are complex exercises in formal arrangements and experimental, non-associative color. A contemporary, Forbes Watson, claimed that Dickinson had no theories about art and that his only desire was to make fine arrangements of forms and color.[42] Yet, especially in his still life paintings, Dickinson was obviously trying to arrive at a synthesis of Cézanne's analytical solutions and the decorative aspects of Oriental art. The opulent color and patterning of Persian ceramics and the linear elegance and perspectival distortions the Impressionists had once borrowed from the Japanese print particularly absorbed him. An early still life in the present exhibition, "Plums on a Plate," 1926, exemplifies this restless fusion of diverse influences. "Still Life with Yellow-Green Chair,"* painted two years later, was his most conclusive achievement of the synthesis he desired. Its sharp-edged table and objects are seen from a variety of almost imperceptibly changing station points, and cast shadows are consistently designed and accented as major structural elements within the composition. In less successful works, however, Dickinson's compulsive designing led to metallic effects and he became the victim of a self-imposed inflexibility.

ABSTRACTION, RETURN AND RENEWAL

In the Forties, Precisionist painting, particularly in the work of Sheeler, Spencer, and Crawford, returned with a new vigor and sophistication to something very much like its initial Cubist-inspired form. Stuart Davis's work has special relevance to this last phase of the Precisionist development. The painting of Davis, Spencer, and Crawford represents three of the most successful American adaptations of the Cubist analytical process. Yet Davis, despite his friendships with Sheeler and Spencer, was never a central figure in Precisionist history as such. While Spencer and Crawford continued to depict industry and technology, Davis was intrigued by a less tangible, more temporary aspect of the American environment, and the uniqueness of his art stems from the strident color and syncopated rhythms of the urban scene. The vivacity and humor of Davis's art has no equivalent in Precisionist painting. Its closest parallel is in the much subtler satire of Demuth, and in spite of stylistic similarities in Davis's work to that of Spencer or Crawford, he has never shared the Precisionist reverence for modern technology.

Davis's painting had a radical effect on Guglielmi. With the passage of time, Guglielmi inevitably moved away from his early subject of the Italian village transferred to New York, for the new generations of Italians were now becoming absorbed as an integral part of the city. Abandoning his painfully evolved quasi-Surrealist style, Guglielmi began to teach himself the lessons of pure abstraction. In this task, he was affected by the work of Spencer, and the later paintings also recall Attilio Salemme's striped canvases of confectionery color. But Davis's bravura style was his real model, and in the mid-Forties Guglielmi began peopling his cityscapes with two-dimensional figures posed under bridges, emerging from subways, drifting along crowded avenues. Yet even in such works as "Third and Icarus," 1950, the Surrealist allegory persists in Guglielmi's newly assimilated abstract technique.

Sheeler's painting in the Forties is similar in its strength and abstract quality to his work of the early Twenties, and the symmetrical pattern of his evolution from a qualified abstraction through photographic realism and back to an even more subtle geometricizing process has already been indicated.

Spencer returned to abstraction in the Forties, but obviously still found it difficult to abandon the secure reference of local subject matter.[43] In "Edge of the City," 1943, for example, an identifiable locale is generalized in the grayed color and geometry of rectilinear shapes. In all his later works, this flat color, lack of modeling, and use of uniform textures for a variety of substances — water, sky, concrete — result in a posteresque quality. He made few sketches for his painting and sometimes used photographs, but his usual method was to transfer important elements of the scene directly to the canvas. Spencer favored a highly centralized composition and achieved this in relatively simple ways: in "Edge of the City" a concentration of high-value color, a radically simplified natural light, brightly illuminates the middle building and ground; in "Two Bridges," 1947, attention is forced to the center through the arbitrary disposition of arcs and diagonals echoing and framing the major forms of bridge and trestle; and the axes of all the objects and planes of "The Desk,"* 1947, either point to or cluster around a centrally placed bottle. "Above the Excavation," 1950, represents Spencer's painting at its most non-figurative limits. But it was not until "Wake of the Hurricane,"* 1951, that his art approached a real dynamism. Here space is pierced by strong diagonals and the building planes are layered and staggered to produce great depth. The value structure, as in most of Spencer's painting, is evenly distributed, hitting almost every interval between black and white. The paint quality is unusually rich and the facets of color are varied enough in size, shape, and placement to produce a scintillating surface.

---

[42]*"Preston Dickinson,"* The Arts, *May, 1924, p. 285.*

[43]*Even the most specific subject matter was still Spencer's point of departure for his exercises in abstraction. He expressed the formalistic Precisionist view when, in describing one of his pictures,* The Silver Tanks, *1949 (not in the exhibition) he wrote, ". . . the painting itself is both* more *and* less *than that observation. Less, in that it is the process of a deliberate limiting of the color scheme and simplification of the shapes, for there is that unavoidable choice that must be made from countless other combinations from this particular subject. More, in that by the selected ordering of the chosen elements of form and color the picture should contain emotional reactions that are not bound by one literal scene." (Undated statement for Downtown Gallery.)*

Demuth   POSTER PORTRAIT OF O'KEEFFE, 1924   The Downtown Gallery

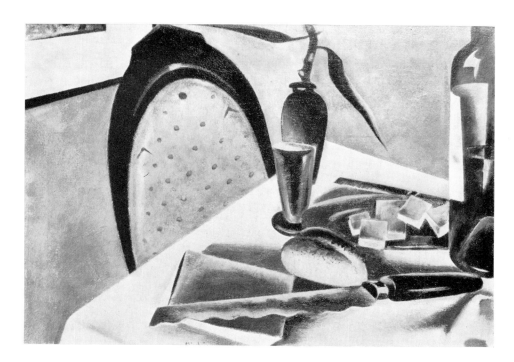

Dickinson   STILL LIFE WITH YELLOW-GREEN CHAIR, 1928   Columbus Gallery of Fine Arts

Spencer   THE DESK, 1948   San Francisco Museum of Art

ABSTRACTION, 1926   Whitney Museum of American Art

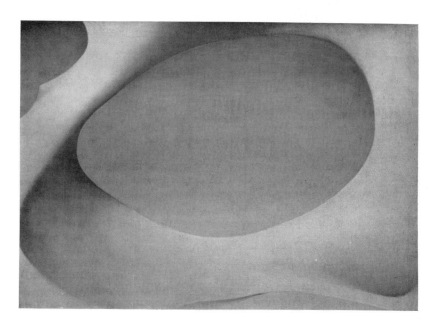

PELVIS SERIES, RED WITH BLUE, 1945   The Downtown Gallery

PATIO WITH CLOUD, 1956   Milwaukee Art Center

Crawford's painting, especially since the mid-Forties, suggests a direction in which the whole Precisionist development might have moved were its artists not so committed to realism. But twenty years earlier Sheeler and Spencer had set the limits of the abstract process in their own work and even when they later returned to its simplifying order chose not to carry their painting to the point where subject was visually no longer apparent. Still, Crawford's work does not necessarily represent an advance over the Precisionist tradition so much as it is a further intellectualization of its formal ideas. His painting of the Forties is in the spirit of the wave of abstraction then gaining strength and characterized by such artists as Karl Knaths, Balcomb Greene, and I. Rice Pereira. The major difference between their painting and Crawford's is that Crawford has consistently been preoccupied with tangible subject matter. True enough, its origins are also in Cubism, but its immediate inspirations are in the structural and mechanical forms themselves, not in speculative essays in pure abstraction. "I speak first of subject matter because for me it is of basic importance."[44] The refinement of his painting approaches that of Demuth's and Sheeler's. Compositionally, his ideas are more varied than Spencer's, whose strength is in the blockiness of his earth-bound forms. Sweeney has used the term "visual understatement" to characterize Crawford's work. "Nothing overstressed. The eye never sated. The onlooker is always left with an appetite for just a slightly warmer tone, for a stronger, a slightly more emphatic line."[45]

Like that of Sheeler and Spencer, whose work his painting most closely resembles, Crawford's development has been gradual and consistent, and his production shows little fluctuation in its evolution and organization. In his non-figurative painting of the past fifteen years, Crawford's approach to abstraction has been toward greater and greater simplification. "Boiler Synthesis,"* 1942, whose subject recalls the shipboard machinery of his sailing days, is treated in an abstract style of extreme linear and coloristic vitality, and its weightlessness and incisive diagrammatic quality are more in the spirit of Léger's early treatments of mechanical subjects than those of the Precisionists.

After World War II, Crawford's painting, still dependent on subject matter, shifted to its most abstract phase. On a commission from Fortune, Crawford was the only artist in a group of observers sent to Bikini in 1946 to witness the atom bomb tests. He executed a series of paintings and drawings based on the ruins of the sacrificial fleet, among them the "U. S. S. Nevada," 1946. Yet with all their patterns of violent color and writhing shapes, derived from the unforgettable chaos of the scene, these pictures were still dominated by the absolute discipline of Crawford's predetermined vision.[46]

The Precisionist leitmotif used in "Grain Elevators, Minneapolis," 1949, is so thoroughly distilled that only a hint of the original structure remains. The chevron-striped supporting beams of the New York elevated and the striated shadows of its trellis and charging trains are energetically evoked in "Third Avenue El,"* 1949. About the process of mixing images Crawford has written, "I am very much interested in a kind of pictorial counterpoint — the juxtaposing of one melody or theme in relation to another, or to several. It is out of this argument or contrast that I believe interest is created in pictorial structure. This must be part of the total plan — I am uninterested in producing the decorative."[47]

FOCUS AND PERSPECTIVE

There can be little question of the magnitude of the Precisionist development. Despite its lack of formal organization or even declared purpose, the collective accomplishment of its artists was, especially in its initial phase, of enormous importance in establishing modern art in this country. But Precisionist limitations as well as achievements are necessarily those of the participants.

Even where the Precisionist has dealt with the tangible subject matter of American countryside or current technology, purely aesthetic considerations always predominate and one is conscious of an intentional distance maintained between the artist and his subject, familiar as that subject might be. The ascetic quality of this painting is reflected in the actual isolation of such artists as O'Keeffe and Sheeler, whose distaste for theories and novelty is implicit in their painting. While the Precisionists early grasped and applied the lessons of Europe to their work, they in turn added little to the great body of speculative thinking about art. The Precisionist current did not deflect or even enter the mainstream of international art, and in spite of its initial reliance on and parallels to European ideas, the Precisionist orientation remains strongly local.

Precisionist art seems concerned with preservation rather than change. Its older artists never entirely shed the conservatism of the academy they rejected, and their evolution has been measured and cautious. Compared to the flamboyant aspirations of the authors and heroes of American literature in the Twenties, the Precisionists' attitude was curiously impersonal. Even in their youth and in spite of their guarded attraction to modern European art,

---

[44]*Quoted by Edward H. Dwight in "Lithographs by Ralston Crawford,"* Art in America, *October, 1955, p. 39.*

[45]*James Johnson Sweeney, introduction,* Ralston Crawford, *Louisiana State University Art Gallery, Baton Rouge, 1950.*

[46]*For Crawford these paintings were a comment on destruction. "They refer in paint symbols to the blinding light of the blast, to its colors, and mostly to its devastating character as I observed it in Bikini Lagoon." (Statement for Downtown Gallery, 1946.)*

[47]*Statement in exhibition catalogue* Ralston Crawford, *Milwaukee Art Center, 1958, p. 11.*

the Precisionists could hardly be described as rebels, and their meditations in paint avoid the disturbing and the sensuous. In this light, the differences between Sheeler's architectural approach and O'Keeffe's organic themes seem minimal.

Despite this, in the Twenties the Precisionist development was a momentous first step in bringing a form of abstract art to an environment still suspicious of European artistic innovations. Although none of the Precisionists was involved in the organized programs and exhibitions of the American Abstract Artists group, formed in 1936, the older movement's importance in pioneering this abstraction cannot be underestimated, and its work clearly anticipated the important American development of abstract-geometric painting of the Forties. If much of the impetus to American abstract painting can be traced to the active presence in this country of such Europeans as Léger, Mondrian, Albers, Moholy-Nagy, Hélion, Ozenfant, and Drewes, the Precisionists had been working systematically and independently along these lines during the years when their deliberate approach to formal problems was a bright note in the morass of regionalism and social realism. As a matter of fact, in spite of its abstract qualities, it was exactly the inherent conservatism of the Precisionist movement that allowed it not only to survive for so long but to flourish so admirably. It could take root because of the single-mindedness of its artists, who always painted with an eye on the American scene and remained faithful to the object.

Martin L. Friedman

Crawford   SHAW'S PROPELLERS #2, 1960   Lent by the artist

BIOGRAPHIES AND CATALOGUE OF THE EXHIBITION

In the artists' biographies, only exhibitions of major importance have been noted. All galleries located in New York unless otherwise indicated. In the listing of painting dimensions, height precedes width.

GEORGE AULT

Born Cleveland, Ohio, 1891. Moved to London 1899. Studied, Slade School of Fine Art, University College, London; St. John's Wood Art School, London. Frequent trips to France. Returned to U.S., 1911; lived in N.J. and N.Y. First American exhibition, Society of Independent Artists, N.Y., 1920. Joined Bourgeois Gallery, 1923. One-man exhibitions, Downtown Gallery, 1926, 1928; New Art Circle, 1927. Moved to Woodstock, N.Y., 1937. Died Woodstock, 1948. Memorial exhibitions, Woodstock Artists' Association Gallery, 1949; Milch Galleries, 1950; Mint Museum, Charlotte, N. Car., 1951; retrospective exhibition, Zabriskie Gallery, 1957.

The Pianist, 1923. Oil on panel, 12 x 16″. Collection of the Nebraska Art Association, Lincoln.

From Brooklyn Heights, 1926. Oil on canvas, 30 x 20″. Collection of the Newark Museum.

Sullivan Street Abstraction, 1928. Oil on canvas, 24 x 20″. Courtesy of the Zabriskie Gallery, New York.

PETER BLUME

Born Russia, 1906. Came to U.S., 1911. Began art studies at age of 12, evening classes, Brooklyn public schools. Evening classes at Educational Alliance, 1921-24; also, Art Students' League, Beaux-Arts, N.Y. Supported self by running subway newsstand, as lithographer's apprentice, work in jewelry factory. First one-man exhibition, Daniel Gallery, 1930. Guggenheim Fellowship, to Italy, 1932; second Guggenheim, 1936. First prize for "South of Scranton," Carnegie International, 1934. Second one-man exhibition, Julien Levy Gallery, 1937. "The Eternal City" rejected from Corcoran Biennial as controversial, 1939. One-man exhibitions at Durlacher Brothers, 1947, 1949, 1954, 1958. Extensive travels to Europe, S. America, Far East, South Seas have provided subjects for recent works. Lives in Sherman, Conn.

White Factory, 1928. Oil on canvas, 20 x 30″. Collection of the Nebraska Art Association, Lincoln.

The Bridge, 1928. Oil on canvas, 30¼ x 24¼″. Collection of Mr. and Mrs. Martin Janis, Sherman Oaks, California.

RALSTON CRAWFORD

Born St. Catharines, Ontario, 1906. Lived in Buffalo, N.Y., 1910-26. Sailor on tramp steamers, Great Lakes and Caribbean. Studied, Otis Art Institute, 1926-27; Pennsylvania Academy of the Fine Arts, Barnes Foundation, 1927-30; Académies Colarossi and Scandinave, Paris, 1932-33; Columbia University, 1933. First one-man show, Maryland Institute of Art, 1934. Extensive teaching and lecturing in American art schools and museums since 1940. U. S. Army Air Force, 1943-45. Witness to Bikini atom bomb tests, 1946. Many photography trips to New Orleans, 1950 to present. Work in lithography and painting in Paris during 1950's. One-man exhibitions, Flint Museum of Art, 1942; Santa Barbara Museum of Art and circuit, 1946; Honolulu Academy of Arts, 1947; Cincinnati Art Museum, 1949; University of Minnesota, 1949; Louisiana State University, 1950; University of Alabama, 1953; Milwaukee Art Center, 1958. Lives in New York.

Boiler Synthesis, 1942. Oil on canvas, 36 x 50″. Lent by the artist.

U.S.S. Nevada, 1946. Oil on canvas, 16 x 22″. Collection of Mr. and Mrs. John J. Carney, New York.

Grain Elevators, Minneapolis, 1949. Oil on canvas, 40 x 32½″. Collection of the Milwaukee Art Center.

Third Avenue El, 1949. Oil on canvas, 29¾ x 40⅛″. Collection of the Walker Art Center.

First Avenue #1, 1954. Oil on canvas, 32 x 40″. Lent by the artist.

New Orleans #7, 1954-56. Oil on canvas, 40 x 28″. Collection of the William H. Lane Foundation, Leominster, Massachusetts.

Shaw's Propellers #2, 1960. Oil on canvas, 24 x 36″. Lent by the artist.

CHARLES DEMUTH

Born Lancaster, Pa., 1883. Studied, School of Industrial Art, Philadelphia; Pennsylvania Academy of the Fine Arts, with Chase, Anschutz, Breckenridge, 1905-10. First trip to Europe, 1907. Studied, Aca-

démies Colarossi, Moderne, Julien, Paris. Second Paris trip, association with Duchamp, "les Jeunes," 1912-14. Many one-man shows, Daniel Gallery, 1914-23; Society of Independent Artists, 1917; Intimate Gallery, 1926, 1929; Morton Gallery, 1929; An American Place, 1931. Trip to Paris, 1921. Included in major Stieglitz group show "Seven Americans" at Anderson Galleries, 1925. Died Lancaster, 1935. Major retrospective exhibitions, Whitney Museum of American Art, 1937; Museum of Modern Art, 1950.

White Architecture, 1917. Watercolor and pencil on paper, 17½ x 11½". Collection of the William H. Lane Foundation, Leominster, Massachusetts.

The Tower—After Christopher Wren, 1919. Tempera on composition board, 23½ x 19⁷⁄₁₆". Collection of the Columbus Gallery of Fine Arts, gift of Ferdinand Howald.

Paquebot, Paris, 1920. Oil on canvas, 24½ x 19⁷⁄₁₆". Collection of the Columbus Gallery of Fine Arts, gift of Ferdinand Howald.

Stairs, Provincetown, 1920. Watercolor and gouache on cardboard, 23½ x 19½". Collection of the Museum of Modern Art, New York, gift of Mrs. John D. Rockefeller, Jr.

Trees, c. 1920. Watercolor on paper, 13¾ x 11¾". Courtesy of The Downtown Gallery, New York.

Modern Conveniences, 1921. Oil on canvas, 25⁷⁄₁₆ x 20¹⁵⁄₁₆". Collection of the Columbus Gallery of Fine Arts, gift of Ferdinand Howald.

Rue du Singe Qui Pêche, 1921. Tempera on composition board, 21 x 16¼". Collection of Mr. and Mrs. Bernard Heineman, Jr., New York.

Nospmas M. Egiap Nospmas, c. 1921. Oil on canvas, 24 x 20". Collection of Mrs. Edith Gregor Halpert, New York.

Poster Portrait of O'Keeffe, 1924. Tempera on composition board, 20½ x 16½". Courtesy of The Downtown Gallery, New York.

Longhi on Broadway (Poster Portrait of Eugene O'Neill), 1927. Oil on cardboard, 36 x 29". Collection of the William H. Lane Foundation, Leominster, Massachusetts.

My Egypt, 1927. Oil on composition board, 35¾ x 30". Collection of the Whitney Museum of American Art, New York.

Poppies, 1929. Watercolor on paper, 14 x 20". Collection of Mrs. Edith Gregor Halpert, New York.

After All . . . , 1933. Oil on composition board, 36 x 30". Collection of the Norton Gallery and School of Art, West Palm Beach, Florida.

PRESTON DICKINSON

Born New York, N.Y., 1891. Studied, Art Students' League, N.Y., with Ernest Lawson, c. 1910. Strong interest in Oriental art, 1913. Worked independently in Europe, primarily France; studied paintings at Louvre and work of Cézanne, 1910-15. Exhibited, Salon des Artistes Français, 1912; belonged to Indépendants; Whitney Studio Club, 1925-26. One-man exhibitions, Daniel Gallery, 1924, 1927, 1930, 1932; Quebec, 1926-27; Smith College Museum of Art, 1934. Returned to Europe, died in Spain, 1930. Memorial exhibition, M. Knoedler & Co., 1943.

Hillside, 1919. Watercolor on paper, 16¾ x 11¹⁄₁₆". Collection of the Columbus Gallery of Fine Arts, gift of Ferdinand Howald.

Factory, 1924. Oil on canvas, 29⁷⁄₈ x 25¼". Collection of the Columbus Gallery of Fine Arts, gift of Ferdinand Howald.

Grain Elevators, Omaha #2, 1924. Pastel and pencil on paper, 13¾ x 9½". Courtesy of The Downtown Gallery, New York.

Plums on a Plate, 1926. Oil on canvas, 14 x 20". Collection of the Museum of Modern Art, New York, gift of Mrs. John D. Rockefeller, Jr.

Still Life with Yellow-Green Chair, 1928. Oil on canvas, 15 x 21". Collection of the Columbus Gallery of Fine Arts, gift of Ferdinand Howald.

Environs of New York, N.d. Pastel on paper, 11½ x 11½". Collection of Norma and John Marin, Jr., New York.

Industry II, N.d. Oil on canvas, 24¾ x 30". Collection of the Whitney Museum of American Art, New York, gift of Mr. and Mrs. Alan H. Temple.

Still Life, Bread and Fruit, N.d. Oil on canvas, 30 x 28⅛". Collection of the Whitney Museum of American Art, New York.

ELSIE DRIGGS

Born Hartford, Conn., 1898. Moved to New Rochelle, N.Y., 1908. Studied, Art Students' League, N.Y., 1919-20. Painted independently, New York, 1921. Trip to Europe and study in Rome with Maurice Sterne; extensive travels throughout Italy, 1922. Exhibited regularly in group shows (including Sheeler, Demuth, Dickinson, Spencer), Daniel Gallery, 1924-32. One-man show, Daniel Gallery, 1928. Yaddo Foundation Fellowship, 1935. New York, 1935-36. One-man shows, Rehn Gallery, 1936, 1938, 1953. Moved to present residence, Lambertville, N.J., 1936. Married to painter Lee Gatch.

Pittsburgh, 1927. Oil on canvas, 34¼ x 40″. Collection of the Whitney Museum of American Art, New York.

O. LOUIS GUGLIELMI

Born Cairo, Egypt, 1906. Early childhood in Italy. To New York, 1914. Tiffany, Yaddo, MacDowell fellowships. Studied, National Academy of Design, 1920-25. Exhibition, New Art Center, Jacques Seligmann, Julien Levy galleries. W.P.A. Art Project, c. 1936. Summer fellowship, MacDowell Colony, N.H., 1932. One-man shows, Downtown Gallery, 1938, 1948, 1951. U.S. Army, World War II. Taught Louisiana State University, 1952-53; New School for Social Research, 1953. Died 1956. Memorial exhibition, Nordness Gallery, 1958.

A Muted Street, 1942. Oil on canvas, 24 x 20″. Collection of Mrs. Edith Gregor Halpert, New York.

One Third of a Nation, 1943. Oil and tempera on wood, 30 x 24″. Collection of the Metropolitan Museum of Art, gift of the New York City Works Progress Administration.

Third and Icarus, 1950. Oil on canvas, 36 x 28″. Collection of the Andrew Dickson White Museum of Art, Cornell University, Ithaca, gift of David M. Solinger.

Fire Escape, 1956. Oil on canvas, 50⅝ x 16¾″. Collection of Mr. and Mrs. M. B. Kaplansky, Toronto.

STEFAN HIRSCH

Born Nuremburg, Germany, 1899. Studied, University of Zurich, 1917-19. Friend of Joyce, Hodler, Dada painters and poets. To U.S., 1919. Studied with Hamilton Easter Field, 1919-22. Joined Bourgeois Gallery, c. 1923. One-man shows, Bourgeois Gallery, 1925, 1927; Downtown Gallery, 1929, 1932; Associated American Artists Gallery, 1941. Mexico, 1931-32. Numerous mural commissions, beginning 1934. Taught, Bennington College, 1934-40; Art Students' League, N.Y., 1941; Bard College since 1942. Lives in New York.

New York, Lower Manhattan, 1921. Oil on canvas, 29 x 34″. The Phillips Collection, Washington, D.C.

EDMUND LEWANDOWSKI

Born Milwaukee, Wis., 1914. Studied, Layton School of Art, 1931-34. Taught in Milwaukee public schools; Florida State University, 1949-54. Represented in major W.P.A. exhibition, Phillips Gallery, 1936. First of several government mural commissions, Hamilton, Ill. post office, 1939. U.S. Army Air Force, World War II. Many commissions for paintings, murals, mosaics. Currently director of Layton School of Art. Lives in Milwaukee.

Ore Freighter, 1948. Oil on canvas, 42 x 30¾″. Collection of the Milwaukee Art Center.

LOUIS LOZOWICK

Born Russia, 1892. Studied, National Academy of Design, 1912-15; Ohio State University, 1915-18. U.S. Army, 1918-19. First of many trips abroad, 1921. Began to paint seriously and exhibit in Berlin, 1921. First major show, International Exhibition, Düsseldorf, 1922. One-man exhibitions, Albert Heller Gallery, Berlin, 1923; Galerie Zak, Paris; J. B. Neumann's Print Room; Stendahl Gallery, Los Angeles; Weyhe Gallery; numerous museums. Société Anonyme exhibition, Brooklyn Museum, 1926. Experimental set design, Goodman Theater, Chicago, 1926. Also graphic artist, author of many articles on art. Lives in South Orange, N.J.

New York, 1926-27. Oil on canvas, 30 x 22″. Lent by the artist.

Oklahoma, 1926-27. Oil on canvas, 30 x 17″. Lent by the artist.

Pittsburgh, 1926-27. Oil on canvas, 30 x 17″. Lent by the artist.

GEORGIA O'KEEFFE

Born Sun Prairie, Wis., 1887. Studied, Art Institute of Chicago, 1904-05; Art Students' League, N.Y., 1907-08; University of Virginia, summer, 1912; with Arthur Wesley Dow, Teachers College, Columbia University, 1914-16. Public school art supervisor, Amarillo, Tex., 1912-14. Taught, Columbia College, S. Car., 1915-16; University of Virginia, summers, 1913, 1915, 1916; West Texas State Normal School, Canyon, Tex., 1916-17. First exhibition, in "291" group show, 1916. First one-man show at "291," 1917. Exhibited, Society of Independent Artists,

N.Y., 1917. Moved to New York, 1918. Exhibited in shows arranged by Stieglitz at Anderson Galleries, 1923-25. Married Stieglitz, 1924. One-man exhibitions, Intimate Gallery, 1926-29; Brooklyn Museum, 1927; An American Place, 1930-46, 1950; Art Institute of Chicago, 1943; Museum of Modern Art, 1946; Worcester Art Museum, 1960. Death of Stieglitz and distribution by O'Keeffe of his collection to museums, 1946. First of several trips to Europe, 1953; to Peru, 1956; around world, 1959. Lives in Abiquiu, N. Mex.

Lake George, Coat and Red, 1919. Oil on canvas, 27 x 23″. Courtesy of The Downtown Gallery, New York.

Dark Abstraction, 1924. Oil on canvas, 24⅞ x 20⅞″. Collection of the City Art Museum of St. Louis.

Abstraction, 1926. Oil on canvas, 30 x 18″. Collection of the Whitney Museum of American Art, New York.

Lake George Barns, 1926. Oil on canvas, 21⅛ x 32″. Collection of the Walker Art Center.

Morning Glory with Black, 1926. Oil on canvas, 35¹³⁄₁₆ x 29¾″. Collection of the Cleveland Museum of Art, bequest of Leonard C. Hanna, Jr.

East River from the 30th Floor of the Shelton Hotel, 1928. Oil on canvas, 30 x 48″. Collection of the Art Museum of the New Britain Institute, New Britain, Connecticut.

New York Night, 1929. Oil on canvas, 40⅛ x 19⅛″. Collection of the Nebraska Art Association, Lincoln.

Ranchos Church, Taos, 1929. Oil on canvas, 24 x 36″. The Phillips Collection, Washington, D.C.

Black, White and Blue, 1930. Oil on canvas, 48 x 30″. Courtesy of The Downtown Gallery, New York.

Horse's Skull with Pink Rose, 1931. Oil on canvas, 40 x 30″. Courtesy of The Downtown Gallery, New York.

Stables, 1932. Oil on canvas, 12 x 32″. Collection of the Detroit Institute of Arts, gift of Mr. Robert Tannahill.

Pelvis Series, Red with Blue, 1945. Oil on canvas, 29¾ x 40″. Courtesy of The Downtown Gallery, New York.

Patio with Cloud, 1956. Oil on canvas, 36 x 30″. Collection of the Milwaukee Art Center, gift of Mrs. Edward R. Wehr.

MORTON SCHAMBERG

Born Philadelphia, Pa., 1881. Studied architecture, University of Pennsylvania, 1899-1903; painting, Pennsylvania Academy of the Fine Arts, 1903-04, 1905-06; with Chase classes to Europe, 1902, 1903, 1904. To Paris, 1906. To Europe with Sheeler, 1908. Shared studio with Sheeler, Philadelphia, 1906-09.

Portrait photography, c. 1913. Represented in Armory Show, 1913. Group show, Montross Gallery (with Sheeler, Stella, Prendergast, Kuhn), 1914. Assembled first exhibition of modern art at McClees Gallery, Philadelphia, 1915. A director, Society of Independent Artists, 1916. Interest in machine subject, 1916. Exhibitions, Independent Artists, 1917, 1920. Died in flu epidemic, Philadelphia, 1918. Memorial exhibition, M. Knoedler & Co., 1919. Represented in first Société Anonyme exhibition, N.Y., 1920.

Machine, 1916. Oil on canvas, 30⅛ x 22¾″. Collection of Yale University Art Gallery, New Haven, Connecticut, Société Anonyme Collection.

Still Life, Camera Flashlight, 1916. Oil on canvas, 24 x 20″. Collection of Dr. and Mrs. Ira Leo Schamberg, Jenkintown, Pennsylvania.

Telephone, 1916. Oil on canvas, 24 x 20″. Collection of the Columbus Gallery of Fine Arts, gift of Ferninand Howald.

CHARLES SHEELER

Born Philadelphia, Pa., 1883. Studied, School of Industrial Art, Philadelphia, 1900-03; Pennsylvania Academy of the Fine Arts, 1903-06. Trips to Europe with Chase, 1904, 1905; with Schamberg, 1908; with family, 1909. Lived in Philadelphia and Doylestown, Pa., 1910-19. Began professional photography c.1912. Exhibited six paintings in Armory Show, 1913. Group shows, Montross Gallery, 1915-17; Forum Exhibition, N.Y., 1916; Society of Independent Artists, N.Y., 1917. One-man exhibition, photographs, Modern Gallery, 1918. Lived in New York, 1919-27. One-man exhibition, paintings and photographs, De Zayas Gallery, 1920; paintings, Daniel Gallery, 1922; Whitney Studio Club, 1924; Downtown Gallery, 1931, 1940, 1946, 1951, 1956, 1958; Arts Club, Chicago, 1932; Fogg Art Museum, 1934; Museum of Modern Art, 1939; Dayton Art Institute, 1944; Addison Gallery of American Art, 1946; Currier Gallery of Art, 1948; Walker Art Center, 1952; University of California, Los Angeles, and circuit, 1954. Lived in South Salem, N.Y., 1927-32; Ridgefield, Conn., 1932-42. Has lived in Irvington-on-Hudson, N.Y., since 1942.

Landscape, 1915. Oil on wood panel, 10½ x 14″. Collection of the William H. Lane Foundation, Leominster, Mass.

Bucks County Barn, 1923. Tempera and crayon, 19¼ x 25½″. Collection of the Whitney Museum of American Art, New York.

Still Life, 1925. Oil on canvas, 24 x 20″. Collection of the California Palace of the Legion of Honor, San Francisco.

Upper Deck, 1929. Oil on canvas, 29⅛ x 22⅛″. Collection

of the Fogg Art Museum, Harvard University, Cambridge, Massachusetts.

Americana, 1931. Oil on canvas, 48 x 36". Collection of Mr. and Mrs. Milton Lowenthal, New York.

Classic Landscape, 1931. Oil on canvas, 25 x 32¼". Collection of Mrs. Edsel B. Ford, Grosse Point Shores, Michigan.

View of New York, 1931. Oil on canvas, 47¾ x 36¼". Collection of the Museum of Fine Arts, Boston.

Rolling Power, 1939. Oil on canvas, 15 x 30". Collection of the Smith College Museum of Art, Northampton, Mass.

Incantation, 1946. Oil on canvas, 24 x 20". Collection of The Brooklyn Museum, J. B. Woodward Memorial Fund.

Manchester, 1949. Oil on canvas, 25 x 20". Collection of the Baltimore Museum of Art, Edward Joseph Gallagher III Memorial Collection.

Aerial Gyrations, 1953. Oil on canvas, 24 x 19". Collection of Dr. and Mrs. Melvin Boigon, New York.

Architectural Cadences, 1954. Oil on canvas, 25 x 35". Collection of the Whitney Museum of American Art, New York.

Midwest, 1954. Oil on canvas, 18 x 32". Collection of the Walker Art Center.

General Motors Research, 1956. Oil on canvas, 48 x 30". Collection of General Motors Research Laboratories, Warren, Michigan.

On a Shaker Theme, 1956. Oil on canvas, 23 x 29½". Collection of Mr. and Mrs. Stephen A. Stone, Newton Center, Massachusetts.

NILES SPENCER

Born Pawtucket, R.I., 1893. Studied, Rhode Island School of Design, 1913-15; instructor in evening classes second year. Studied, Ferrer School, N.Y., with Bellows and Henri, 1915. Lived in Ogonquit, Me., winters in N.Y., 1917-21; Europe, 1921-22. Joined Daniel Gallery, Whitney Studio Club, 1922-23. First one-man show, Daniel Gallery, 1925; second, 1928. Europe, 1928-29. Joined Downtown Gallery, 1930; one-man show, 1947. Died 1952. Memorial exhibition, Downtown Gallery, 1952; major retrospective traveling exhibition, Museum of Modern Art, 1954.

City Walls, 1921. Oil on canvas, 39⅜ x 28¾". Collection of the Museum of Modern Art, New York.

New York, 1922. Oil on canvas board, 17½ x 13½". Collection of Mrs. Edith Gregor Halpert, New York.

The Cove, 1922. Oil on canvas, 28 x 36". Collection of the Newark Museum.

Interior, Still Life, 1925. Oil on canvas, 35 x 35". Collection of Mr. and Mrs. Edward S. Greenbaum, New York.

Green Table, 1930. Oil on canvas, 50 x 40". Collection of the Whitney Museum of American Art, New York.

Edge of the City, 1943. Oil on canvas, 25 x 29". Collection of Mr. Joseph H. Hirshhorn, New York.

Apartment Tower, 1944. Oil on canvas, 34 x 24". Collection of the Whitney Museum of American Art, New York, gift of Mr. and Mrs. Alan H. Temple.

In the Cabin, 1947. Oil on canvas, 47⅝ x 38½". Courtesy of The Downtown Gallery, New York.

The Two Bridges, 1947. Oil on canvas, 28½ x 45½". Collection of Mr. and Mrs. Roy R. Neuberger, New York.

The Desk, 1948. Oil on canvas, 24 x 32". Collection of the San Francisco Museum of Art, gift of the Women's Board.

Erie Underpass, 1949. Oil on canvas, 28 x 36". Collection of the Metropolitan Museum of Art, Arthur H. Hearn Fund, 1950.

Above the Excavation, 1950. Oil on canvas, 48 x 32". Collection of the William H. Lane Foundation, Leominster, Massachusetts.

Wake of the Hurricane, 1951. Oil on canvas, 30¼ x 36½". Collection of the Walker Art Center.

STUART DAVIS

Born Philadelphia, Pa., 1894. Moved to East Orange, N.J., 1901. Studied, Robert Henri's art school, N.Y., 1910-13. Exhibited with Independents, 1910, 1916. Five watercolors in Armory Show, 1913. First one-man show, Sheridan Square Gallery, 1917. Numerous one-man shows, Downtown Gallery, since 1927. "Eggbeater" series, early experiments in abstraction, 1928. Paris, 1928. Teaching includes Art Students' League, N.Y., New School for Social Research. W.P.A. Art Project, 1933. Guggenheim Fellowship, 1952. One-man exhibitions include Ardsley Gallery, Brooklyn, 1918; Newark Museum Association, 1925; Whitney Studio Club, 1926; Whitney Studio Galleries, 1929; Cincinnati Modern Art Society and Indiana University, 1941; Museum of Modern Art, 1945; Baltimore Museum of Art, 1946; Little Studio, N.Y., 1954; Walker Art Center and circuit, 1957. Lives in New York.

Eggbeater #3, 1928. Oil on canvas, 25 x 39″. Collection of the William H. Lane Foundation, Leominster, Mass.

JOSEPH STELLA

Born Muro Lucano, Italy, c. 1879. To New York, 1896. Studied, Art Students' League, N.Y., 1900; New York School of Art, with Chase, 1902. To Europe, 1909-13; first contact with Futurists. Several works in Armory Show, 1913. A director of Society of Independent Artists, 1916. Exhibited with Independents, 1917; Whitney Studio Club, 1921. One-man shows, Bourgeois Gallery, 1918, 1920; Naples, 1929; Valentine Gallery, 1931, 1935; Cooperative Gallery, Newark, 1937; Newark Museum, 1939; Associated American Artists Gallery, 1941; M. Knoedler and Co., 1942; ACA Gallery, 1943; Egan Gallery, 1946. Died New York, 1946.

The Gas Tank, 1918. Oil on canvas, 40½ x 30″. Collection of Mr. and Mrs. Roy R. Neuberger, New York.

BIBLIOGRAPHY

The following is a selected bibliography which, chronologically arranged, documents the Precisionist movement through a sampling of the most pertinent commentary on the movement. Exhibition catalogues are indicated by an asterisk.

1921 HARTLEY, MARSDEN. *Adventures in the Arts,* New York, Boni and Liveright, 1921 (O'Keeffe)

1923 CRAVEN, THOMAS. "Charles Sheeler," *Shadowland,* 8:11+, Mar. 1923

WATSON, FORBES. "Charles Demuth," *The Arts,* 3:77-8, Jan. 1923

1924 ROSENFELD, PAUL. *Port of New York,* New York, Harcourt, Brace and Co., 1924 (O'Keeffe)

WATSON, FORBES. "Preston Dickinson," *The Arts,* 5:285, May 1924

1925 WATSON, FORBES. "A Note on Niles Spencer," *The Arts,* 8:167-69, Sept. 1925

1926 GOODRICH, LLOYD. "New York Exhibitions," *The Arts,* 9:342-49, June 1926 (Ault)

PARKER, ROBERT A. "The Classical Vision of Charles Sheeler," *International Studio,* 84:68-72, May 1926

PHILLIPS, DUNCAN. *A Collection in the Making,* New York, E. Wehye, 1926

WOLF, ROBERT. "Louis Lozowick," *The Nation,* 122:186, Feb. 17, 1926

1927 BLUEMNER, OSCAR. "A Painter's Comments," *Georgia O'Keeffe,** New York, The Intimate Gallery, 1927

BOURGEOIS, STEPHAN. *Exhibition of Paintings by Stefan Hirsch,** New York, Bourgeois Galleries, Inc., 1927

GALLATIN, ALBERT E. *Charles Demuth,* New York, William Edwin Rudge, 1927

HIRSCH, STEFAN. *A Catalogue of Paintings,** New York, Bourgeois Galleries, Inc., 1927

LOZOWICK, LOUIS. "The Americanization of Art," *Machine Age Exposition,** p. 18-19, New York, *Little Review* et al., 1927

MATHER, FRANK J., JR. et al., eds. *The American Spirit in Art,* XII, New Haven, Conn., Yale University Press, 1927

MUMFORD, LEWIS. "O'Keeffe and Matisse," *The New Republic,* 40:41-2, Mar. 2, 1927

O'BRIEN, FRANCES. "Americans We Like," *The Nation,* 125:361-62, Oct. 12, 1927 (O'Keeffe)

1928 KALONYME, LOUIS. "Georgia O'Keeffe; A Woman in Painting," *Creative Art,* 2:xxxv-xl, Jan. 1928

1929 CLURMAN, HAROLD. "Photographs by Paul Strand," *Creative Art,* 5:735-38, Oct. 1929

MC BRIDE, HENRY. "Water Colours by Charles Demuth," *Creative Art,* 5:634-35, Sept. 1929

STELLA, JOSEPH. "The Brooklyn Bridge (A Page of My Life)," *Transition,* 16-17:86-8, June 1929

1930 KOOTZ, SAMUEL M. *Modern American Painters,* New York, Brewer and Warren, Inc., 1930

MANNES, M. "Niles Spencer, Painter of Simplicities," *Creative Art,* 7:58-61, July 1930

1931 KOOTZ, SAMUEL M. "Preston Dickinson," *Creative Art,* 8:339-41, May 1931

LUHAN, MABEL D. "Georgia O'Keeffe in Taos," *Creative Art,* 8:406-10, June 1931

MURRELL, WILLIAM. *Charles Demuth,* New York, Whitney Museum of American Art, American Artists Series, 1931

ROSENFELD, PAUL. "After the O'Keeffe Show," *The Nation,* 132:388-89, Apr. 8, 1931

ROSENFELD, PAUL. "Charles Demuth," *The Nation,* 133:371-73, Oct. 7, 1931

WELLMAN, RITA. "Pen Portraits: Charles Demuth, Artist," *Creative Art,* 9:483-84, Dec. 1931

1932 BRACE, ERNEST. "Charles Sheeler," *Creative Art,* 11:97-104, Oct. 1932

CAHILL, HOLGER. "American Art Today," *America as Americans See It* (Fred J. Ringel, ed.), p. 243-66, New York, Harcourt, Brace and Co., 1932

GODSOE, ROBERT U. "Peter Blume—A New Vision," *Creative Art,* 11:11-15, Sept. 1932

1933 *Index of Twentieth Century Artists,* New York, College Art Association, 1933-1937, 4 vols

1934 BARR, ALFRED H., JR. and HOLGER CAHILL, eds. *Art in America in Modern Times,* New York, Reynal and Hitchcock, 1934

BLUME, PETER. "After Superrealism," *The New Republic,* 70:338-40, Oct. 31, 1934

FRANK, WALDO et al., eds. *America and Alfred Stieglitz: A Collective Portrait,* New York, Doubleday, Doran and Co., Inc., 1934

1935 CAHILL, HOLGER and ALFRED H. BARR, JR., eds. *Art in America, A Complete Survey,* New York, Reynal and Hitchcock, Inc., 1935

1936 AMES, WINSLOW. "A Portrait of American Industry," *Worcester Art Museum Annual,* 2:96-8, 1936-37

CORTISSOZ, ROYAL. "From Old Venetians to Various Moderns," *New York Herald Tribune,* Jan. 12, 1936, sec. 5, p. 10 (O'Keeffe)

HARTLEY, MARSDEN. *Georgia O'Keeffe — A Second Outline in Portraiture,** New York, An American Place, 1936

LANE, JAMES W. "Charles Demuth," *Parnassus,* 8:8-9, Mar. 1936

MUMFORD, LEWIS. "The Art Galleries: Autobiographies in Paint," *The New Yorker,* 11:48-9, Jan. 18, 1936 (O'Keeffe)

1937 PHILLIPS, DUNCAN, foreword. *Preston Dickinson Exhibition,** New York, M. Knoedler and Co., 1937

MILLIKEN, WILLIAM M. "White Flower by Georgia O'Keeffe," *The Cleveland Museum of Art Bulletin,* 24:50-3, Apr. 1937

1938 MC BRIDE, HENRY. *Charles Demuth Memorial Exhibition,** New York, Whitney Museum of American Art, 1938

"Reviving a Memory," *The Art Digest,* 12:20, Apr. 15, 1938 (Dickinson)

1939 COATES, ROBERT M. "The Art Galleries," *The New Yorker,* 15:70-1, Oct. 1939 (Sheeler)

GENAUER, EMILY. "Charles Sheeler in One-Man Show," *New York World Telegram,* Oct. 7, 1939, p. 34

LANE, JAMES W. "Of Sheeler's Immaculatism," *The Art News,* 38:10, Oct. 7, 1939

WILLIAMS, WILLIAM CARLOS, introduction. *Charles Sheeler,** New York, Museum of Modern Art, 1939

O'KEEFFE, GEORGIA. "About Myself," *Exhibition of Oils and Pastels,** New York, An American Place, 1939

1940 "Portfolio Power," *Fortune,* 22:73-83, Dec. 1940 (Sheeler)

1941 *A New Realism: Crawford, Demuth, Sheeler, Spencer,** Cincinnati, Cincinnati Art Museum, 1941

1942 LEE, SHERMAN E. "The Illustrative and Landscape Water Colors of Charles Demuth," *Art Quarterly,* 5:158-75, Spring, 1942

MELLQUIST, JEROME. *The Emergence of an American Art,* New York, Charles Scribner's Sons, 1942

1943 MILLER, DOROTHY C. and ALFRED H. BARR, JR., eds. *American Realists and Magic Realists,** New York, Museum of Modern Art, 1943

RICH, DANIEL C. *Georgia O'Keeffe,** Chicago, Art Institute of Chicago, 1943

RILEY, MAUDE. "Dickinson Surveyed," *The Art Digest,* 17:19, Feb. 15, 1943

SOBY, JAMES T. "Peter Blume's Eternal City," *Museum of Modern Art Bulletin,* 10:1-6, Apr. 1943

1944 GUGLIELMI, O. LOUIS. "I Hope to Sing Again," *Magazine of Art,* 37:173-77, May 1944

WATSON, ERNEST W. "Niles Spencer," *American Artist,* 8:14-17, Oct. 1944

1946 "Bikini: Documentary Photographs, Abstract Paintings and Meteorological Charts," *Fortune,* 34:156-61, Dec. 1946

BROWN, MILTON W. "Cubist-Realism: An American Style," *Marsyas,* 3:139-60, 1946

1947 BORN, WOLFGANG, *Still-life Painting in America,* New York, Oxford University Press, 1947

COATES, ROBERT M. "Out of the Past," *The New Yorker,* 23:87-96, Nov. 22, 1947 (Spencer)
5 Prodigal Sons: Crawford, Davis, Demuth, Levi, Sheeler,* Philadelphia, Coleman Art Gallery, 1947

HESS, THOMAS B. "Spencer," *Art News,* 46:37, Nov. 1947

1948 HITCHCOCK, HENRY R. *Painting Toward Architecture,* New York, Duell, Sloan and Pearce, 1948

MALONE, MRS. JOHN E. "Charles Demuth," *Papers of the Lancaster County Historical Society,* 52:1-18, 1948

1949 CORWIN, CHARLES. "Best Buys in Paintings at A.C.A. Galleries," *New York Daily Worker,* Feb. 4, 1949, p. 12 (Sheeler)

LOWENGRUND, M. "George Ault 1891-1948," *The Art Digest,* 23:20, Sept. 15, 1949

RUGGLES, JOHN. *George Ault Memorial Exhibition,* Woodstock, N.Y., Woodstock Art Gallery, 1949

1950 FAISON, S. LANE, JR. "Fact and Art in Charles Demuth," *Magazine of Art,* 43:122-28, Apr. 1950

RITCHIE, ANDREW C. *Charles Demuth,* New York, Museum of Modern Art, 1950

SWEENEY, JAMES J., introduction. *Ralston Crawford,* Baton Rouge, Louisiana State University, 1950

POLLITZER, ANITA. "That's Georgia," *Saturday Review of Literature,* 33:41-3, Nov. 4, 1950

1951 BAUR, JOHN I. H. *Revolution and Tradition in Modern American Art,* Cambridge, Mass., Harvard University Press, 1951

1952 CAHILL, HOLGER. "Niles Spencer," *Magazine of Art,* 45:313-15, Nov. 1952

1953 FREEMAN, RICHARD B. *Ralston Crawford,* Birmingham, University of Alabama Press, 1953

1954 HAYES, BARTLETT H., JR. and FREDERICK S. WIGHT; foreword by William Carlos Williams. *Charles Sheeler, A Retrospective Exhibition,* Los Angeles, University of California, 1954

MC BRIDE, HENRY. "An Elegant American Painter," *Art News,* 53:20-1+, Mar. 1954 (Spencer)

1955 BROWN, MILTON W. *American Painting from the Armory Show to the Depression,* Princeton, N. J., Princeton University Press, 1955

CHANIN, A. L. "Charles Sheeler: Purist Brush and Camera Eye," *Art News,* 54:40-1, Summer 1955

DWIGHT, EDWARD H. "Lithographs by Ralston Crawford," *Art in America,* 43, 3:40-1, 1955

1956 RICHARDSON, EDGAR P. *Painting in America,* New York, Thomas Y. Crowell Co., 1956

1957 BAUR, JOHN I. H. et al., eds. *New Art in America, 50 Painters of the 20th Century,* Greenwich, Conn., New York Graphic Society, 1957

1958 BRY, DORIS. "Alfred Stieglitz: Photographer," *Alfred Stieglitz,* Washington, D.C., National Gallery of Art, 1958

DWIGHT, EDWARD H. *Ralston Crawford,* Milwaukee, Wis., Milwaukee Art Center, 1958

FOLTZ, JOSEPHINE K. *Charles Demuth, Lancaster Artist,* unpublished paper delivered to Cliosophic Society, Lancaster, Pa., Apr. 25, 1958

MUNRO, ELEANORE C. "Georgia O'Keeffe," *Art News,* 57:38+, Mar. 1958

DAVIS, STUART, foreword. *O. Louis Guglielmi Memorial Exhibition,* New York, Nordness Gallery, 1958

1959 COHEN, GEORGE M. "Charles Sheeler," *American Artist,* 23:32-7+, Jan. 1959

CRAVEN, GEORGE M. "Sheeler at Seventy-Five," *College Art Journal,* 18:136-43, Winter 1959

1960 ANDREWS, EDWARD D. "The Shaker Manner of Building," *Art in America,* 48, 3:38-45, 1960

ARNASON, H. H. "The New Geometry," *Art in America,* 48, 3:54-61, 1960

FRIEDMAN, MARTIN L. "The Precisionist View," *Art in America,* 48, 3:30-7, 1960

RICH, DANIEL C. *Georgia O'Keeffe,* Worcester, Mass., Worcester Art Museum, 1960

SCULLY, VINCENT J., JR. "The Precisionist Strain in American Architecture," *Art in America,* 48, 3:46-53, 1960

WATSON, ERNEST F. "The Art of Ralston Crawford," *American Artist,* 24:47-51+, Apr. 1960

Colophon:

5300 of these catalogues were printed by the
Colwell Press of Minneapolis for the Walker Art Center
in November of 1960.

Type Composition by Dahl & Curry, Inc., Minneapolis.

Engravings by The American Engraving Company, Minneapolis.

The text paper is Warren's Cumberlund Dull, Basis 100,
cover is Warren's Cameo Brilliant Cover Dull Finish, Basis 80.

The text type is Trade Gothic and Trade Bold, notes are
Times Roman and the display types are Radiant Bold Condensed
and Venus Medium Extended.